AFTER
THE
FAST

AFTER THE
FAST

Phillip M. Sinaikin, M.D.
with Judith Sachs

DOUBLEDAY
New York   London   Toronto   Sydney   Auckland

Published by Doubleday, a division of
Bantam Doubleday Dell Publishing Group, Inc.
666 Fifth Avenue, New York, New York 10103

Doubleday and the portrayal of an anchor
with a dolphin are trademarks of Doubleday,
a division of Bantam Doubleday Dell
Publishing Group, Inc.

Height/Weight chart (pages 30–31) adapted from Metropolitan Life's *Height &
Weight Tables for Men and Women*. Used by kind permission of the
Metropolitan Life Insurance Company.

Flavors to Replace Salt chart (pages 76–77) reprinted from *Low Cholesterol,
Low Sodium: Restricted Meal Plans* by Agnes Gordon Fry, Copyright © 1979
Robert J. Brady Company. Reprinted with permission of Appleton & Lange.

Low-Fat Eating chart (pages 78–79) reprinted with permission of the *Newark*
(New Jersey) *Star-Ledger*.

Library of Congress Cataloging-in-Publication Data

Sinaikin, Phillip M., 1951–
After the fast / Phillip M. Sinaikin, with Judith Sachs. —1st ed.
p. cm.
1. Obesity—Prevention. 2. Reducing—Psychological aspects.
3. Reducing exercises. I. Sachs, Judith, 1947–   . II. Title.
RC628.S624   1990
613.7—dc20   89-17097   CIP

Design by Richard Oriolo

ISBN 0-385-26758-4
Copyright © 1990 by Phillip M. Sinaikin, M.D.
All Rights Reserved
Printed in the United States of America
January 1990
First Edition
BG

I owe my wife Ronnie so very much,
including credit for many of the ideas
in this book. So to my best friend and
adviser, my wife, and to our three lovely daughters
Jamie, Benay, and Shara, I lovingly
dedicate this book.

Acknowledgments

I would like to thank my teachers, peers, and friends at Boston University School of Medicine, Maricopa Medical Center, West Georgia College, and Fair Oaks Hospital for all of their help and support through the years.

Additionally, I would like to thank the scientists and researchers who have turned their critical eyes to the field of obesity and disproved the many myths and false ideas about weight control that have been guiding our thinking for far too long.

To my editor Judy Kern for shepherding me so smoothly through the publishing process, and finally, many thanks to Susan Ginsburg for her undying support.

Contents

PREFACE viii

ONE **Keeping It Off:**
The After the Fast Program 3

TWO **Food and Exercise:**
A Complementary Exchange 13

THREE **First Stage—**
Weeks One Through Three 25

Step I. How to Eat Again—Tapering Off from
Your Fast 25

Step II. How to Start Your Exercise Program 40

Step III. Hunger and Satiety—A New Way to Think
About Eating 56

FOUR **Second Stage—**
Weeks Four Through Eight 72

Step IV. What to Eat Now—The Portion-Controlled
Maintenance Program 72

Step V. Exercise Exchanges—Resetting Your
Setpoint 94

Step VI. The Psychology of Weight Maintenance 111

FIVE **Final Stage—**
Week Nine Through the
Rest of Your Life 131

Step VII. No Forbidden Foods—How to Eat for
the Rest of Your Life
Without Counting Calories 131

Step VIII. The Exercise Challenge—Working Toward
Goals 145

Step IX. Keys to New Self-Esteem 156

INDEX 175

Preface

America, as a nation, is getting fatter. The National Health and Nutrition Examination Survey reported recently that from 1971 to 1974, 28.8 million adults were diagnosed as overweight. But during the next charted period, from 1976 to 1980, that figure had risen to 34 million.

Why should this be so? Why should informed consumers who care about living longer and better eat too much of the wrong things? One reason, of course, is that the food is there for the taking. We're reaping the advantages of an opulent lifestyle—and we're paying for it with our health. Because markets overflow with tasty, appealing items of every variety, most Americans are tempted by high-calorie, high-fat foods that are detrimental to their health.

We also spend a great deal of time in sedentary activities —sitting in front of the computer or the television set, at board meetings or at the dining room table. It's become common practice in our competitive, workaholic society to put in long hours at the office, grabbing meals and snacks when we can. But the notion of a healthy mind in a healthy body is more relevant than ever in an age when we expect so much of ourselves. Although it's become a challenge to lead a healthy, natural life—one in which you eat only when you're hungry, exercise as much as you can, and sleep contentedly at night—this is the goal you should be striving for.

If you're just coming off a liquid-protein fast, you've probably been going on diets—and going off them—most of your adult life. The purpose of this book is to help you to maintain, in a *natural* manner, the weight you've just lost. To show you that you never have to diet again. To teach you *how* to eat and not just *what* to eat. To encourage you to become active and involved in your body instead of ignoring it or abusing it.

After the Fast is intended to put you *permanently* in touch with the sense of self-esteem and pride, the feeling of physical accomplishment, that your current weight loss has produced. After all, as you open to the first page of this book, you are at an extraordinary advantage—you are already at or approaching your goal weight. You've overcome the influence of past failed diets and doubting spouses and friends. You've dealt with family meals, business lunches, and parties while never touching a bite of solid food yourself. Your willpower, self-control, and determination to do something very good for yourself are accomplishments you can be enormously proud of.

You are undoubtedly wary of eating now, because you haven't consumed solid food in months. You probably regard food as a problem to be solved, a difficult adversary to be beaten. Something to be avoided whenever possible because it's too tempting to consider.

After the Fast is going to change that misguided attitude. When you've mastered the principles of maintaining your weight, you'll be able to see food as a source of nutrition, enjoyment, and social intercourse. You'll be what I term an unrestrained eater, who is able to consume whatever you want *when you are hungry*, and able to stop *when you are full*.

You will be able to maintain your new, post-fast weight forever. Not only that, you will feel physically better than you've ever felt, and learn to manage your eating so that you will never have to count another calorie, never have to turn away from foods you really love.

Now that your fast is over, the feast of life lies ahead of you. Enjoy!

PHILLIP M. SINAIKIN, M.D., M.A.
Millburn, New Jersey

AFTER THE FAST

O N E

Keeping It Off: The After the Fast Program

If you've been overweight for most of your adult life, you may feel that your body is a burden, something to haul around, something to work on. Your physical being may be a liability you are always struggling to overcome. You may consider yourself a physical failure in a world that so highly values success.

But, strange to say, for many people it may be even harder to *accept* success. To have worked so hard for so long, and to have thereby achieved a particular goal, may leave you feeling empty rather than elated. You've finally lost the weight—so now what do you do? Has it made a difference in your life? Have you learned anything about yourself by accomplishing this feat? And finally, now that you've reached your goal, where do you go from here?

If you're just coming off a long fast, it can be difficult—even painful—to confront your new body and begin to deal with it. It can be frightening to consider the cost, both physical and psychological, of returning to normal eating. Even when you can see the results of your phenomenal efforts on the scale, you may look at yourself in the mirror and say, but is this *really* me? Do I like it? How can I learn to live with it? And how do I really know that tomorrow, or the next day, I won't slip up and suddenly become fat again?

What Fasting Has Done for You—And What It Hasn't Done

Of course, you *had* to lose the excess weight you were carrying. You were in grave physical danger if you were "morbidly obese"—that is, weighing a hundred pounds or more over your ideal body weight. You were still at risk if you were moderately obese and had, say, thirty to fifty pounds to lose. Obesity impairs both cardiac and pulmonary functions; it causes an increase in blood pressure, impairs glucose tolerance, and creates gall bladder and orthopedic problems. It is an independent risk factor for atherosclerotic heart disease, and can also cause emotional problems.

Though we all know people who can drop ten or twenty pounds if they have to with little or no effort, having a great deal of weight to lose is an entirely different problem. As we know, on traditional diets the body reaches a plateau after a certain point, and weight loss slows or even—in many cases—stops. With a liquid-protein fast, on the other hand, you are guaranteed to lose continually if you stick to it. After all, when your body is reduced to a state of semi-starvation, it can't remain at a plateau—it must continue to lose weight.

In one thirteen-week study of liquid-protein fasters, men lost an average of 4.6 pounds per week; women an average of 3.1. They were delighted to find that not only were the pounds falling off, but they were also reaping additional physical benefits; they noticed a reduction in hypertension, diabetes, and raised blood fats (hyperlipidemia). And the most important and appealing factor of this diet is that *they were hardly ever hungry.*

When you're on a traditional reduced-calorie diet, given a range of food alternatives, even a cookbook full of possibilities, the variety and tastiness of the dishes you can prepare for yourself often whet your appetite too much. On such a diet you experience both mouth hunger (when you want to eat because it tastes good) and true stomach hunger (a physiological condition in which intestinal contractions bring on hunger pangs). Eating 1,000 calories a day never makes you feel "full"—neither your taste buds nor your stomach are satisfied. You may begin with your "allowed" portion but go on to experiment with more, because it's delicious and because you're still hungry. And when you've "blown your diet" anyway, what harm could a piece of chocolate cake do? Your mouth is still hungry even when your stomach is full because you've been depriving yourself for so long.

A fast works the opposite way, by removing all possible appetite stimuli. It's understood that you will have only one taste in your mouth for months—that of a slightly sweet milkshake in a variety of predictable flavors. Fasting eliminates the dreaded hunger pangs that make most diets unbearable simply because a fasting diet is necessarily monotonous—you *know* that nothing except that drink or bland small meals will pass your lips for weeks or even months. The reason so many successful fasters regress when they finally come off the fast is their initial confrontation with the variety and tastiness of food they can eat. Going from total boredom to almost total freedom in their eating unleashes a monstrous hunger that can't be controlled—except by gorging and bingeing on everything that is guaranteed to gain the weight back again.

In addition to this problem fasting also has side effects. Remember, your body has no way of understanding that you are simply trying to lose weight. When you stopped ingesting food, your body reacted as if you were dying—there was a famine in the land. When there's no fuel coming in, the body resorts to borrowing from its already existing fat and muscle stores. It reacts in a self-protective way by slowing or shutting down all its major systems in order to conserve energy and preserve life. Additionally, a long-term faster may experience constipation, cold intolerance, dizziness and lightheadedness, dry skin, and fatigue. Hair loss is a real problem for some. And there may be psychological damage that lasts for months after the fast ends.

An interesting experiment, conducted by Ancel Keys of the University of Minnesota, was done during World War II on the effects of semi-starvation. Keys wanted to simulate wartime deprivation, to see how it would affect a community. He and his colleagues isolated thirty-six men of average weight and put them on a daily diet of 3,500 calories for three months. During this time the men made friends in the group, did maintenance work, engaged in physical activity, took courses, and held weekly meetings. Then, for the next three months, their rations were cut in half. Though 1,750 calories a day is certainly not an insignificant amount of food, it was considerably less than what they had been eating.

The men uniformly grew irritable and argumentative, friendships broke apart. They lost interest in activities they had previously enjoyed, and spent most of their time on their cots, conserving energy. They were ravenous at mealtime, and although the food was bland and unpalatable they would dawdle over it, taking as much time to eat as possible. After three months of this, at the end of the study, the men were allowed to eat whatever they wanted. They set to with a vengeance, consuming about 5,000 calories daily. And they were *still* hungry.

In addition to losing a lot of fat during the experiment, they had lost muscle (lean tissue); it was not until long after the program ended, when they'd been eating freely for nine months, that they regained it. All the men eventually returned to their original balance of muscle and fat, but their obsession with food—as in the case of many fasters coming off several months of a liquid diet—lasted long after they were back to their normal weights.

Current research indicates that keeping off the weight lost through fasting is exceptionally difficult. Data from the Optifast Program at Beth Israel in Newark, New Jersey, indicate that 10 percent of those who began the program dropped out immediately; 25 percent lasted only three weeks of the allotted time. Of the group that remained in the program, 68 percent never reached their goal weights and, in fact, tended to gain back *all* their lost weight. The final 32 percent achieved their goal weights, but very few were able to keep it off for more than eighteen months.

Let's look at these grim statistics again, in accordance with their reported sex ratios:

- 78 women and 22 men come to the introductory lecture
- 4 women and 6 men finish the program and keep the weight off for eighteen months

What happened to the determination, the will power, the incredible desire never to be fat again? The point here is that most of the group never learned anything from their experience. They were able to lose weight when they stayed on the liquid-protein diet—but naturally they had to stop fasting at a certain point and start living with food again, something that few of them apparently found easy to do. They returned to their old habits and regained their weight. What is significant here is that:

Fasting will take weight off, but only a changed attitude toward eating will keep it off.

Fasting and Metabolism

I can't count the number of times people have told me, "I'm fat because I have a slow metabolism and there's nothing I can do about it." Technically, this can be true. Some obese people do tend to have a lower metabolic rate than thin people. When they're dieting—and particularly when they're fasting—their metabolism decreases even further.

Let's clarify for a moment what we mean by *basal metabolism*. This is the energy required to keep the body functioning while at rest. Basal metabolism uses up 50 to 70 percent of our daily energy expenditure just keeping the heart beating, the lungs functioning, and all the organs in the body working efficiently. Why does the basal metabolism rate drop when you go on a diet?

Mankind has survived throughout the centuries through both feast and famine. Because of the regulatory nature of our metabolism, we're able to survive on either a great deal or very little. When we are forced to cut down on our caloric intake, our bodies use fuel more efficiently and cut down on our energy requirements. The men in the Keys study, for example, slowed their activity rate substantially when their calorie intake was cut in half. Their basal metabolic rate slowed down to help them survive until the fuel supply increased. The greater the caloric decrease, and the longer the body has to make do with less, the greater the drop in metabolic rate. I think you can now see why a three-month fast would make the body's daily energy requirements plummet.

The curious part of the body's reaction to a fast is that *it does not recover its pre-fast metabolic rate when eating begins again*; therefore, fewer calories are needed to put weight on *after* a fast than were needed prior to it. So if you do not make changes in the way you eat and deal with food, it will take only a few months of eating the way you did before the fast to gain back what you've lost.

To summarize, at the end of a fast you have:

- a slowed metabolism
- a sense of long-term deprivation
- no greater awareness of why your eating habits—not the particular foods you eat or don't eat—have gotten you to the point of needing to fast.

If you are coming to the end of a long-term fast, you weigh a lot less than you used to. This is wonderful, in and of itself. But if you look at the failure rates of so many post-fasting patients, your justifiable pride at having reached goal weight may start to crumble. The fasting portion of your program did nothing to teach you why you failed with food in the past, and hasn't given you a clue as to what to do to maintain your new weight throughout the rest of your life. Additionally, most follow-up programs insist that you stick to a low-calorie diet forever, thus continuing to deny and deprive yourself. But the very reason you had to fast in the first place was that *low-calorie diets never worked* for you before. Why should they be any different now?

The Program
for Lifelong Weight
Maintenance

I don't believe in diets. I don't think that anyone should go through life counting mouthfuls and reading box-tops. Naturally you want to stick as close as you can to a diet of foods low in fat and cholesterol, one that is good for your heart and your longevity. And you also need to give your body a daily workout to raise your metabolic rate and to put you in touch with exactly how well this wonderful machine can function—how good it can make you feel.

But there's no reason, if you're on a good maintenance

program of eating and exercise, that you can't eat foods that give you pleasure—because food, aside from being a source of nutrition, should also be a source of pleasure.

The nine-step program I want you to follow is a gradual means of:

1. easing back into the acceptance of food.
2. beginning or increasing a daily exercise regimen.
3. changing preconceived attitudes about yourself and the way in which you eat.

The three interlocking facets of this program—eating, exercise, and positive self-image—are going to ensure your success in lifelong weight maintenance.

Weeks 1–3. The first stage of our program reintroduces you to eating on a gradual basis, allows you to begin to get in touch with your new body through exercise, and teaches you to recognize when you are hungry and when you are full.

Step I. Taper Off Your Fast
Learn how to reduce your liquid-protein intake and begin to introduce solid food into your diet.

Step II. Make a Daily Date with Yourself to Exercise
Learn that only by exercising will you be able to burn more calories and achieve a general fitness level that will help you to maintain your weight.

Step III. Hunger and Satiety
Learn to understand how to judge for yourself—without arbitrary dietary rules—when to eat and when to stop.

Weeks 4–8. The second stage of our program brings you to the intermediate level of maintenance. Here, you learn to eat, without counting calories, three portion-controlled solid meals and two snacks. You choose two or possibly more types of exercise to use in combination. And you begin to question your old beliefs about dietary restriction and freedom.

Step IV. What to Eat

Learn to eat a varied, portion-controlled diet based on your goals for further weight loss or maintenance.

Step V. Exercise Exchanges

Discover that you can change your metabolism by practicing a five-day-a-week aerobic schedule.

Step VI. The Psychology of Weight Maintenance

Begin to examine and modify your own attitudes and beliefs about "fat" and "thin" and what eating and exercise have to do with the way you think about your self-worth.

Week 9—the rest of your life. The final stage of our program uses eating, exercise, and self-esteem as tools for the experienced post-faster. Because you will know how to eat, you will no longer have to worry about what to eat. Because you'll be back in touch with your body as a result of exercising, you'll be able to set some really challenging—but realistic —physical goals for yourself. And because you will have learned to like where you are and what you're doing for yourself, you won't be as tough a taskmaster if you do happen to slip a few pounds over your goal weight.

Step VII. No Forbidden Foods

Become able to eat whatever you like, within the boundaries of your hunger and satiety levels.

Step VIII. The Exercise Challenge

Set yourself a previously impossible physical goal—a marathon, a tournament, a black belt—that will allow you to enjoy the fruits of your new body strength.

Step IX. Keys to Self-Esteem

Master the art of liking yourself as you are and as you will be, and allow yourself to be imperfect, but fine.

This program, once established, is effortless to maintain. You will have lived with yourself long enough as a practicing unrestrained eater, as a vital athlete, and as a coping human being to see that any other way of handling your weight is artificial and unnatural.

You will find, as you make this program a part of you, that you will achieve your own balance, your own method of using the program. The beautiful part of eating to live instead of living to eat is that it is a natural, human way to behave. It makes sense. When you stop thinking about food as dangerous because it leads to bingeing, when you no longer see exercise as a painful method of self-torture, when you know how to eat comfortably and sensibly, you will have reached the final goal of the program: You will stop worrying about your weight.

In the next chapter, we'll set down the basic ground rules for eating and exercise and show you just how they make a lifetime marriage dedicated to your well-being.

DIGESTIBLES

1. Just because your metabolism has slowed down as a result of fasting is no reason to believe you can't raise it, and thus lower your risk of putting the lost weight back on.

2. Your body feels good when you use it; exercise is not abuse; it is natural and healthy.

3. When you feel "in danger" around food, realize that you are bigger and stronger than anything you could eat. You can make decisions; food cannot.

4. If you approach eating and exercise in a natural, realistic manner, you will never feel as if you're going out of your mind with hunger and deprivation.

T W O

Food and Exercise: A Complementary Exchange

When you get out of bed and walk down the hall to the bathroom, when you reach for your toothbrush, when you take off your pajamas and get dressed for the day, you're expending calories. If you do those activities at a normal pace and then go downstairs and eat a couple of doughnuts and drink two cups of coffee with cream for breakfast, you will have not only replaced the calories you just burned—you will have added about 300 more!

But suppose you got up and put on some sweats, and then stretched your limbs for about fifteen minutes and did a few jumping jacks in place. Then you pulled on your socks and sneakers and went for a brisk walk. When you finished your

two-mile jaunt, you then sat down to a breakfast of cereal
and skim milk or an apple and a bran muffin. Or maybe, as
a treat, you ate one doughnut.

By beginning your day with half an hour of mild aerobic
exercise, you would have accomplished the following:

- burned calories by directly expending energy
- raised your overall metabolic rate
- accelerated your cardiac and pulmonary activity, which
  improves general body fitness
- decreased your hunger
- reduced your tension level by starting the day with a
  period of time spent doing something good for you
- helped increase your HDL cholesterol (the good component of cholesterol) and lowered the harmful fats in
  your blood
- allowed yourself the option of eating something you enjoy, thus satisfying your mouth hunger as well as your
  stomach hunger without creating a calorie excess and
  gaining weight

All this, just from a two-mile walk? Absolutely.

The physical and psychological benefits of exercise are
enormous. If you look at an animal—unless it's been do-
mesticated and pampered beyond the point of no return—
you'll see that exercise is vital to its well-being. A cat will
jump from chair to couch, chase a ball, pounce on a bug,
even roll over with exaggerated muscle extension. A dog may
lie around for a good portion of the day if he's alone, but
will leap up at the sight of a leash, drag his owner around
the corner, even attempt to rush up a tree if he sights a
squirrel. He will probably not consume everything you put
in his bowl, but will regulate his intake to his daily expenditure of energy and calories burned.

We can do exactly the same thing, if we choose to be good
to ourselves. After all, we too are animals and the human
body was intended to be active. Prior to the Industrial Rev-

olution, our lives were spent in pursuits such as farming, chopping wood, scrubbing floors, riding horses. The sedentary life style of twentieth-century men and women is unnatural and harmful—and our bodies let us know that we're neglecting them by manifesting all sorts of medical problems that miraculously seem to vanish once we begin a daily exercise program and sensible eating.

Restrained and Unrestrained Eating

It's a very curious fact that obese people, as a rule, do not eat more than thin people do. On average, they eat the same or less than their skinny counterparts. What seems to separate the two groups is the way the food is consumed.

Obese people, in particular those who are chronic dieters, tend to be *restrained* eaters. They eat according to a running mental checksheet of indulgences and deprivations, not according to what their body needs. They're always aware of how much they've consumed and how much more they'd really like to eat—if they weren't so worried about being fat. Some will restrain themselves from eating all day, then feel ravenous at night and reward themselves with a gigantic meal, consuming more calories than they probably would have if they'd eaten at regular intervals throughout the day. Others tend to eat by the clock—if it reads 12:30 or 6 P.M., they *know* it's time for them to be hungry, so they prepare a meal and eat it.

Because restrained eaters classify their daily food intake as being either "bad" or "good," once they've given themselves the leeway to take one taste of a "bad" food, they feel they've completely blown their diet—so they might as well go right ahead and gorge themselves. They tell themselves that they can start being good again tomorrow, but for now, it just doesn't matter. Nothing matters except the taste of that forbidden food (which they will, of course, never allow themselves again). That one piece of chocolate or slice of pie releases an unchained food maniac who can't stop.

And they generally don't compensate for eating by exercising—and this is the biggest contributing factor in putting weight back on after a diet or a fast.

Naturally thin people, on the other hand, tend to be *unrestrained* eaters. They eat when they're hungry and stop when they're full. They eat more on days when they're more physically active and thus burn more energy—and therefore more calories. They eat what they like, when they want it; but because they know they can always have it again tomorrow or next week, they don't have to go hog wild. They may eat enormous quantities of something they really relish, but the next day they may leave most of their food on the plate.

Unrestrained eaters don't necessarily adhere to a strict mealtime—if they're hungry at 3 P.M., that's when they'll eat. They may then skip dinner, or have just a late evening snack. If they're going to a wedding one afternoon and a buffet dinner the next, they'll probably cut back on what they consume for two days after the big meals. The amazing thing is that they will *naturally* regulate their weekly food intake so that it comes out balanced with their energy requirements. They will probably have selected requisite amounts from all the four food groups and a few items from non-nutritious indulgence foods. But the difference between a restrained and an unrestrained eater is that, in the case of the latter, the indulgences won't be looked on as "bad." They're just considered extras—and they'll probably be burned off with exercise, anyway.

Restrained eating—monitoring every bite, as you do on a diet—is what gets you in trouble. Unrestrained eating—consuming calories when the body needs them—is what nature intended.

Exercise
and Metabolism

Do obese people tend to exercise less than thin people? Probably they do, because when you're carrying all that excess baggage it's more cumbersome to get up and sit down, to run up and down stairs, to sprint to the bus. A fat body that's out of condition is also going to suffer more when put under the stress of exercise. If you haven't gotten up off the couch all fall and suddenly you have to go out and shovel the snow from your front walk, you're asking for trouble. Under these circumstances, the stress on your heart and lungs can lead to some real problems.

But if fat people have slower metabolic rates than thin people, isn't it natural that they have trouble expending a lot of energy? Doesn't a fat body naturally crave to move slowly and deliberately? Actually, no. But it might be "defending" a larger fat store than its thin counterpart.

What Is
Your Setpoint?

Scientists have posited that each body has a setpoint—that is, a predetermined, desired fat store. This is based on the idea that the body comes with a preset internal thermostat that will adjust to changes in intake and maintain a certain percentage of fat.

If you set your home thermostat at 68°, it stays at that temperature. If the weather changes, and it becomes cold outside, the mechanism compensates by turning itself on and adjusting the temperature upward. As soon as the house is 68 again, it turns itself off.

Our bodies also have compensatory mechanisms to maintain a certain percentage of fat. When you diet below your body's natural setpoint of fat, your metabolism slows down to compensate; also, certain enzymes that regulate fat deposition come into play, and the hypothalamus in the brain starts sending urgent messages about hunger and appetite to the rest of the body. Your inner thermostat tends to keep you at a percentage of fat that's comfortable for your particular body. It's very hard to change your setpoint, which is determined by both genetic and environmental factors.

How can you figure out what your setpoint is? Think back to a one- to two-year period in your adult life when you weren't consciously trying to control your weight. Wherever you hovered on the scales—give or take ten pounds—is your natural setpoint. This is a range of weight that can be comfortably maintained with a reasonable intake of food and a normal activity level. It's very often the case that a person's setpoint is above the ideal body weight prescribed for him or her in life insurance tables. Some people, who feel they must be model-skinny or look great in a pair of skin-tight pants, might be fighting a losing battle against their own biology. They are probably below their natural setpoint.

If you think back to diets you've been on in the past, you will probably recall that once you began being less vigilant about the number of calories you were consuming each day, your weight insidiously rose again to its pre-diet level, give or take a few pounds. It wasn't as if you were suddenly eating massive quantities, and yet there you were back again at that same depressing weight. It was more depressing because you really thought you'd done pretty well on the diet.

If you've been on a fast for months, you are probably quite a bit below your natural setpoint. To be able to remain at or near this goal, you are going to have to reset your setpoint to a lower weight.

There is only one sensible way to do this—by exercising.

Woodsmen in the Canadian Northwest are very hungry when they come in from a day of logging; so are Amish farmers after a day working in the fields. The gigantic meals they consume, loaded with calories, would stagger a dieter in his tracks. Not all of these people have naturally low set-points. Why is it, then, that they can eat what they want when they want and still maintain their weight?

The more physical energy you expend, the more you can eat without gaining weight. If you elevate your energy level, you can also elevate your calorie consumption.

Hunger is one mechanism the body uses to get back to its natural setpoint. But metabolism is another. If your body is working at a slower rate because you've been fasting, then you must consciously work to raise your metabolism so that you can keep your setpoint low.

Setpoint and metabolism are both variables that can change if you increase your body's activity level.

Metabolic
Effects of Exercise

You expend a lot of energy while you're exercising, which means you're burning calories. Look at the following equations:

1. When calories consumed (food) = calories expended (exercise and basal metabolism), then weight stays the same.
2. calories consumed > calories expended = weight gain.
3. calories consumed < calories expended = weight loss.

PROVEN: The more you exercise, the more you can eat and not gain weight.

Remember that you drastically lowered your metabolism by fasting. When you cut back on the calories you consumed each day, your body reacted in a self-protective manner. It lowered its energy requirements because it simply wasn't getting enough fuel to keeping going at a nice, normal clip.

Now that your fast is over, your metabolism is at its lowest point ever. You've got to pay attention to the fact that as soon as you start eating solid food again, you're going to start putting on weight. The first pounds to come back after any diet come back as fat—not muscle. This means that it's particularly important to start a *daily* exercise program that will raise your metabolism and keep it high.

As you begin to burn calories by walking, jogging, riding a bicycle, or taking an aerobics class, you'll be able to consume calories more freely and still keep the weight off. You'll also be helping to reset your setpoint downward.

You have to expend an awful lot of energy to equalize the effects of eating, but the effects of daily exercise are *cumulative*, which is the important point here. Technically, you'd have to run two hours to work off a McDonald's burger, fries, and a Coke. That's not really doable for the average person. But if you exercise for just *half an hour* daily on a regular basis you will raise your overall metabolism so that a McDonald's meal will have a much smaller impact on your weight.

Endorphin Release

Endorphins are hormonal substances in the brain that are naturally released during exercise. You've heard of the "runner's high"—this is the experience many athletes have at the peak of their physical exertion. Researchers have discovered that somewhere around the midpoint of a vigorous workout, the exerciser will begin to feel a kind of euphoria, a sense of pleasure and purpose. Colors seem brighter, smells sweeter, your body stronger and lighter. Anything seems possible. This is the result of endorphin release.

Significant physical exercise brings with it its own reward. Not only does it make sense in terms of raising metabolism, supporting unrestrained eating, and developing better body fitness and image; it also offers the psychological benefit of a wonderful sense of peace and well-being. Though some researchers worry about the "body cultists"—exercisers so addicted to staying in peak physical condition that all else pales in comparison—we really don't have to be too concerned about that problem at this point in a program of weight-maintenance. Of all the addictions possible, exercise is usually the least harmful. It might even be called a positive addiction.

How Exercise Makes
You Feel About Eating

If you're concerned about your body, if you really care how it looks and feels, you're going to have a much greater stake in what you put into it. There is a nice compensation the body makes after working out. After a good exercise session, you are simply less hungry than you were before exercising. In Step III of our program we discuss how to figure out whether you're hungry or not hungry—and, most important, how to know you've reached your level of *satiety*, a sense of satisfaction with what you've consumed. The interesting thing is that after exercise, you'll be able to enjoy a more complete level of satiety—and be satisfied with less food!

How Exercise Makes
You Feel About Yourself

When you begin an exercise program, particularly if you've never done anything active before, you may feel embarrassed, ridiculous, frustrated, and discouraged. Coming off a fast, you may feel more fatigued (as a result of your lowered metabolism); and the very idea of going for a two-mile walk in a brisk wind at six-thirty in the morning before your family is awake may make you want to roll over and go back to sleep.

But the point is that if you had the incentive and guts to stay on a liquid-protein fast for three or four months, you cannot refuse your body the opportunity of continuing to enjoy your good care and attention. As you will see by looking in the mirror, you are thin—near or at your goal weight—but chances are your muscles are out of shape. Only exercise is going remold your reduced body. What you're going to do now is to build lean body tissue that will enhance your appearance, strength, and fitness.

Remember that muscle is more metabolically active than is fat. This means that while you are on a regular exercise regimen, your body will burn more calories doing anything and everything, from preparing a salad to trying on a new dress to sleeping. Because your basal metabolism is going to be working faster, it's going to be expending more energy just keeping your body functional. And energy expended means calories burned, which means further weight loss or maintenance.

You'll probably be surprised to find that, once having started on a regular daily exercise program, you may willingly perform physical activities you never considered before. You may climb the stairs in your apartment house instead of taking an elevator. You may walk to the newspaper stand instead of taking the car. You may agree to shoot a few baskets with your teen-age son, or lope along beside your four-year-old while she rides her bike. These novel choices allow you not only to see the world from a different perspective, but to burn more calories as well.

Once your energy level has increased, you'll find that exercise also puts you at a social advantage. Whereas you might have stayed inside before because you were ashamed of your body, now you'll want to show it off. When you agree to a morning jog with your neighbor, or set a tennis date with your boss, you're expanding your social horizons. The time you may spend networking in this way will be almost as beneficial as the extra calories you'll expend.

Then there are the innumerable psychological benefits of

exercise that researchers have discovered. Just a few worth mentioning are the following:

1. a reduction in tension and stress
2. more adequate sleep and rest
3. increased ability to concentrate; increased mental energy
4. improved self-image and more self-confidence
5. greater interest in health-related activities, including healthier eating habits

Could there be any greater rewards? Ask yourself if, prior to your fast, you enjoyed your work and had boundless energy to put into it—and still more left over for your family and friends. I wouldn't be surprised if your answer was a resounding *no*.

Most likely, the only pleasurable things you can recall from before your fast were sedentary activities and the taste of food—which is a reward we all enjoy. But the pain of what too much of the wrong kinds of foods did to you undoubtedly raised your stress level and cut you off from other people. What you did by fasting was to make room for all the other rewards I've just mentioned—as well as for food. And now, food doesn't have to be the sole reason for your being. It can take its rightful place alongside exercise, work, play, sex, travel, friends, and family, as one facet of a well-rounded life.

DIGESTIBLES

1. Instead of wasting time making calorie charts and counting mouthfuls, you can use that time constructively burning calories by walking, jogging, swimming, etc.

2. When you exercise daily, you can enjoy food and not get fat.

3. When you've finished exercising, the body will crave something to drink. This is an excellent time to have a few glasses of water—which will help stave off your appetite.

4. When you've finished exercising, you'll have a good, warm feeling in your body—a sense that you've renewed yourself and are ready to tackle something else. This is one meaning of the word *satiety*—a sense of complete satisfaction.

5. When you exercise—no matter what else happens during the day—you've already done something nice for yourself.

THREE

First Stage—
Weeks One Through
Three

Step I. How to Eat Again—
Tapering Off from Your Fast

You've been incredibly dedicated to your fast, whether you had thirty or one hundred pounds to lose. You went either to your doctor or to the market on a regular basis and purchased your liquid-protein diet formula then, as though steak and potatoes or chocolate cake with a scoop of ice cream were nothing more than distant memories, you downed your four or five drinks daily. You were a good pupil, you did your homework, and it paid off handsomely. You are now practically at your destination—within five or ten pounds of your goal weight—a place you never thought you'd visit again in your life.

It's time to start thinking about solid food. You can do it! This time, you can do it the right way. Because I'm going to teach you *how to eat.*

Why You Should
Make a Commitment to
Stop Fasting

An obsession about *not* eating can be just as harmful to your health as an obsession about eating. Simply because you were thoughtless about food in the past is no reason to assume that, the minute you begin taking in solid food again, you'll get yourself right back up to the weight you were at before you fasted. Remember, it takes time to gain a lot of weight, just as it does to lose a lot of weight. And you simply cannot continue to avoid food for the rest of your life. I want you to start thinking about eating as a natural, healthful phenomenon instead of an uncontrolled need that must be fulfilled.

You and your doctor or you and your conscience went into the fasting experience thinking about an end-point, a realistic weight goal you wanted to reach. What I'm asking you to do is to taper off from your fast when you're within five or ten pounds of that goal. Once you're on the AFTER THE FAST program of eating and exercise, you'll be able to lose more weight if you choose to, though of course at a slower rate than when you were fasting.

You may currently be considering the idea of fasting until you are below your ideal weight. Then, at least, you think to yourself, if I go back to food and blow my maintenance diet a couple of times, it won't be the end of the world. I'll have given myself a buffer so that I can eat and not worry too much. The worst that would happen is that I'd get back up

to my ideal weight and then go back on the fast for a few
more weeks.

I counsel you very strongly against this plan. It is a glaring
example of the thinking of a *restrained eater*, whose complete
approach to food has to do with being either on or off a diet.
The very notion of "blowing the diet" and risking only gaining
back up to your ideal weight, is a wrongheaded one, for these
reasons:

- It allows you to prolong the fast and not even consider
  how you're going to approach eating solid food.
- It allows you to accept the possibility of bingeing after
  your fast is over.
- It doesn't take into consideration your body's natural
  signals for hunger and satiety—which will eventually be
  the control elements in your lifelong maintenance plan.

Stop, then, *before* you've lost all the weight you want to.
The very fact that you've achieved this extraordinary reducing feat means that you will have no trouble losing the rest.
And the method by which you're going to lose it will be based
on a realistic assessment of food.

How to Eat

If you've been under a doctor's care for the duration of your
fast, you probably got a lot of information about what to eat
and when to eat. What I'd like you to concentrate on is *how
to eat*.

What do you mean? you'll ask. Eating is automatic, isn't
it? You just take the food and put it in your mouth and chew
it and swallow it.

Not at all—not if you've been a restrained eater throughout
your adult life. If you're accustomed to monitoring every
mouthful, and especially if you're coming off a long fast, you
are probably terrified of the prospect of ingesting solid food.
Because it was food that got you into this situation in the
first place.

When you think about how to eat, your thoughts undoubtedly go like this:

• I should do it at regular mealtimes.
• I should do it when everyone else is eating.
• I should do it quickly so I'll get finished and won't have to think about it—until the next meal.

Wrong! That's not how to eat at all. The way to maintain weight and to stay physically healthy and psychologically sound, in terms of food, is to become an *unrestrained eater*—someone who eats when hungry and stops when full. Someone who doesn't engage in mental debates about every bite; who doesn't punish him- or herself for eating a little too much one day, and doesn't bother rewarding him- or herself for missing a meal on another day. (The meal was missed because there was something more interesting or crucial to do than eat at that particular time.)

Restrained eating is learned behavior. It stems from a certain personal discontent and is reinforced by society's unfortunate dictum that "people can never be too thin or too rich." It is a cruel method of punishment because it makes you simultaneously your own enforcer and your own victim. Living your life on a rigid diet doesn't admit for celebrations, special splurges, true enjoyment of the experiences that get you together with other people to share a meal. You can become a real sourpuss, living on a perennial diet and always having the feeling that "they can and I can't—it's not fair."

Like any learned behavior, restrained eating can be unlearned. It takes practice and concentration at first, but believe me, with each day and each meal it gets easier. When you've relearned the natural sensations of hunger and satiety, you'll never have to think about being on a diet—or blowing a diet—again. Those words will vanish from your vocabulary.

Your Ideal-Weight Goal

You are currently consuming five fasting drinks, or four fasting drinks and one meal (chicken or fish and a salad), totaling less than 1,000 calories per day. You aren't having many problems with hunger right now, because your body and mind have adjusted to life without food. There's a kind of comfort in each fasting meal, with the realization that it's getting you closer to your goal. You are probably not tempted by real food at all.

If you're not under a physician's care, I'm going to help you make the very important decision about when to stop your fast. (If you are under a physician's or nutritionist's care in a fasting program you might consider discussing these recommendations with him or her.)

The goal weight you set should be rational and reasonable, and in accordance with your previous weight history. Look at the table of ideal body weights on pages 30–31. This is a standard life insurance table that is used as a guidepost in all dieting literature. Though it may be applicable to those who have never struggled with being overweight, it's not necessarily on the mark for long-term fasters.

As you try to figure out where you should be for your height, sex, and body size, ask yourself:

Have I been significantly overweight since childhood or adolescence?

If the answer is "yes," your weight goal *at this point* should be 20 percent above the table's estimate. If the answer is "no," ask yourself:

In my adult life, have I ever been at my ideal weight? If so, have I been able to maintain it for any appreciable amount of time without starving myself?

If you've never been at your ideal weight as an adult, but had no problem with weight during childhood or adolescence, your weight goal at this point should be 10 percent

WOMEN

Height	Small Frame	Medium Frame	Midpoint Reference	+10%	+20%	Large Frame
4'10"	102–111	109–121	115	127	138	118–131
4'11"	103–113	111–123	117	129	140	120–134
5' 0"	104–115	113–126	120	132	144	122–137
5' 1"	106–118	115–129	122	134	146	125–140
5' 2"	108–121	118–132	125	138	150	128–143
5' 3"	111–124	121–135	128	141	154	131–147
5' 4"	114–127	124–138	131	144	157	134–151
5' 5"	117–130	127–141	134	147	161	137–155
5' 6"	120–133	130–144	137	151	164	140–159
5' 7"	123–136	133–147	140	154	168	143–163
5' 8"	126–139	136–150	143	158	172	146–167
5' 9"	129–142	139–153	146	161	175	149–170
5'10"	132–145	142–156	149	164	179	152–173
5'11"	135–148	145–159	152	167	182	155–176
6' 0"	138–151	148–162	155	170	186	158–179

MEN

Height	Small Frame	Medium Frame	Midpoint Reference	+ 10%	+ 20%	Large Frame
5' 2"	128–134	131–141	136	150	163	138–150
5' 3"	130–136	133–143	138	152	166	140–153
5' 4"	132–138	135–145	140	154	168	142–156
5' 5"	134–140	137–148	142	156	170	144–160
5' 6"	136–142	139–151	145	160	174	146–164
5' 7"	138–145	142–154	148	163	178	149–168
5' 8"	140–148	145–157	151	166	181	152–172
5' 9"	142–151	148–160	154	169	185	155–176
5'10"	144–154	151–163	157	173	188	158–180
5'11"	146–157	154–166	160	176	192	161–184
6' 0"	149–160	157–170	163	179	196	164–188
6' 1"	152–164	160–174	167	184	200	168–192
6' 2"	155–168	164–178	171	188	205	172–197
6' 3"	158–172	167–185	174	191	209	176–202
6' 4"	162–176	171–187	179	197	215	181–207

above the table's estimate. But if the answer is "yes"—if you've maintained your ideal weight as an adult without starving yourself—use the table's ideal weight as your goal. Unless you've been told by a doctor that you are particularly small- or large-boned, use the medium-frame weights as your reference point.

You do not have to live your life by someone else's arbitrary rulings. The weight that's right for you may not look or feel right on a friend who's the same height and build. Remember that your setpoint is difficult to move around, particularly when you're just coming off a fast.

The good news is that 10 percent or even 20 percent over "norm" is going to be a realistic and attainable figure for you that will still contribute greatly to your better health and appearance. Once you're fully engaged in the AFTER THE FAST program and have begun eating three solid meals and exercising daily, you may be able to set yourself a lower weight goal.

I think you should be pleasantly surprised by the numbers—the 10 percent and 20 percent allowances I've built in are considerably more generous than the traditional expectations for your height and build. The important thing is that they are *attainable* and *maintainable*. Your goal is to keep to a manageable weight for the rest of your life, not to match up with some degree of perfection set out in a fashion magazine.

Remember that the significant health risks of obesity usually apply only to those who are 30 percent or more above their ideal weight; this means that 20 percent is a safe margin for you unless you suffer from other health conditions that are aggravated by excess weight. If you're at risk for hypertension, diabetes, or high blood cholesterol, you and your physician should set a lower goal weight for you that can be reached gradually on this maintenance program.

Tapering Off

What I want you to do is eliminate one liquid-protein drink every four days until you are eating three solid meals and two solid snacks per day. If you feel shaky about going back to solids this quickly, remember that your body will tell you if you're overdoing. After weeks or months on a purely liquid diet, it would be almost impossible for you to start overeating at this point. You'd suffer so greatly from attacks of diarrhea, gas, pain, and nausea, that you'd have to moderate your intake or feel miserable most of the time.

I want you to take away one drink every four days in the following order:

1. dinner
2. breakfast
3. lunch
4. midafternoon snack
5. evening snack

Each time you eliminate a liquid-protein meal, you will substitute in its place a solid meal composed of 100-calorie amounts from the four major food groups: proteins, dairy products, cereals and grains, and fruits and vegetables.

Women will select three portions for breakfast, lunch, and dinner (900 calories), and two snacks of 100 calories apiece. Men will have their choice of four portions for each meal (1,200 calories), and two snacks of 100 calories apiece.

If you don't already own a diet scale, purchase one now. If you aren't already taking multivitamin pills, begin to do so on a daily basis.

You might want to plan your menus in advance, filling out a chart like the following sample with your next day's choices. This will eliminate the dread of having too many possibilities to pick from, and will start you thinking clearly about exactly what and when you're eating.

LUNCH AND DINNER CHOICES

Proteins

Fish (broiled or baked, no butter)	3 oz.
Shrimp, scallops, or lobster	4 oz.
Tuna fish, water-packed	3 oz.
Canned salmon	⅓ cup
Chicken or turkey without skin	2½ oz.
Red meat (lean ground beef or veal), trimmed of all visible fat, not marbled	2 oz.

Dairy Products

Lowfat cottage cheese	½ cup
Nonfat yogurt, plain	½ cup
Skim milk	8 oz.
Hard cheese	I oz.

Cereals and Grains

Whole wheat bread	I slice
English muffin	½
Pita bread	I slice
Beans	½ cup
Noodles, plain	½ cup

Fruits and Vegetables

Most vegetables, raw or cooked	I cup
Salad (with vinegar or lemon)	I cup
Baked potato	I medium

| Whole fruits (apple, banana, pear, plum, peach, melon) | I medium piece |
| Strawberries, grapes | I cup |

BREAKFAST CHOICES

Proteins

| Egg (poached, scrambled in Pam, hard- or soft-boiled) (*no more than 3 eggs a week*) | I extra large |

Dairy Products

Skim milk	8 oz.
Buttermilk	8 oz.
Nonfat yogurt, plain	½ cup
Lowfat cottage cheese	½ cup

Cereals and Grains

Bagel	½
Whole wheat or white toast	I slice
Unsweetened dry cereal	I cup
Unsweetened hot cereal	½ cup

Fruits

| Grapefruit or cantaloupe | ½ |
| Whole fruits | I medium |

SNACK CHOICES

Rice cakes	3 pieces
Unsalted crackers	6
Hard cheese	I oz.

Whole fruits	I medium
Strawberries or grapes	I cup
Popcorn (air-popped)	3 cups

DAILY TOTALS:

WOMEN	MEN
1,100 calories	1,400 calories

SAMPLE MENU—EIGHTH DAY

Breakfast	I cup cereal, I cup skim milk, I banana
Lunch	Liquid-protein drink
Dinner	8 ounces shrimp, baked potato (This is two 4-ounce shrimp portions, mix and match as you like)
Midaft. snack	Liquid-protein drink
Evening snack	Liquid-protein drink

Why These Foods Now?

Think about what's going on in your body and your mind as you come off a long fast. Physically, all your systems have been severely deprived. Your intestinal tract—your digestive system and bowels—have been in a state of suspended animation. You can't awaken them violently, or you'll wreak some real havoc. If you went back to three solid meals and two snacks a day immediately, you might suffer massive bloating, diarrhea, and gall bladder problems, not to mention heartburn and gas. It's essential that you wean your body back to food slowly and introduce bland, easy-to-digest foods first. But the most important reason for starting with the foods I've listed is that they are boring and dull, lacking the pizzazz a true gourmand craves.

The greatest danger in returning to food after a fast is that you will unleash uncontrollable hunger when you begin eating. Hunger is proportional to the stimulating and enticing quality of the food you eat. If the food is boring, you won't be ravenous for it.

Many fasters fear that all they have to do is taste one bite of anything, from a carrot stick to a boiled egg, and they'll be unable to stop eating. They fear that they may unleash such terrible hunger that they'll start gorging themselves and immediately put all the weight back on. This simply isn't true—you must trust yourself and believe that you can eat food again and *not gain weight*.

Trying out high-calorie, well-spiced meals, however, is a risk that can lead you to rapidly regain a lot of weight. Remember that your metabolism is at its lowest point ever, and so the pounds that you put on now will go on fast.

Eventually, when you have reached Step VII in the advanced stage of this maintenance program, you will be able to eat all your favorite foods all of the time. But right now, I want you to concentrate on tapering off from your fast with run-of-the-mill, ordinary, one-star, nutritious but nonstimulating, *boring* foods.

If you are practically falling asleep in your plate from lack of interest while on this temporary eating plan, you can switch around from time to time. For example, you can have three proteins for dinner (women have a choice of any three portions for any meal), or two grains and two vegetables (men have a choice of four at each meal). But don't be too creative, and don't use spices and seasonings to give the food flavor.

We are trying to keep these first meals as boring as possible so as not to stimulate your appetite.

Eating at Home

For the duration of your fast you've dealt with watching everyone around you eating while you dutifully downed your liquid-protein drink. Now, the challenge changes. Whereas you may have found it relatively easy to watch others around you eating food while you were prohibited from eating, it might be more difficult to consume bland, boring food while they are enjoying the enticing meals you've cooked for them.

This is a temporary situation. Right now, you're getting your body in shape for the natural, normal course of events, which is ingesting three delicious average-sized meals and maybe a couple of snacks, just like everyone else.

Think of yourself as a child just starting out, learning about how your body feels at different times of day. Really give some thought to your physical and psychological reactions to eating. They're going to be crucial in the next stage of maintenance.

Eating Out

There is no reason why you shouldn't be allowed to go to a nice restaurant with your spouse, family, or friends while you're tapering off from your fast. Some of the biggest rewards of a meal include the enjoyment you can derive from the company of others, going out to a lovely place, being pampered, getting dressed up, and so on. It's not what you're putting into your mouth that you'll remember a week later, but rather the experience itself. If you can look at going to a restaurant as a social event instead of an opportunity for eating yourself into a frenzy, you'll begin to pay more attention to the other rewards of eating out.

Here are a few helpful hints to assist you when you're

surrounded by the fragrance of roast lamb and tempted by the sight of the pastry cart coming around the bend.

1. Have one of your complex carbohydrate snacks (the rice cakes, crackers, or popcorn) on the way to the restaurant. This way, you won't be so hungry when you order.
2. Plan what you're going to eat before you get to the restaurant. Try not looking at the menu at all. This takes away the danger of being tempted by the descriptions of food preparations that are frequently more appetizing than the food itself.
3. Make your instructions clear to the waiter or waitress. You'll find it's helpful to say aloud, "I'll have a salad, broiled fish, and a plain baked potato, and please keep the coffee coming. That's all I'll be having."

How to Monitor Your Weight

It was impossible not to lose weight while you were fasting. You had the satisfaction of standing on the scale in your doctor's office or at home and seeing those pounds drop away, day by day, week by week. The culmination of your fast was probably that moment when you stepped on the scale and realized that you had done something you never thought possible—gotten within range of your ideal weight.

But as soon as you begin ingesting solid food, there is a possibility that you may stay on a plateau for a while, or even gain a couple of pounds. *Don't panic—this is normal, and again it's temporary.* Fasting was not a natural state for your body, and it slowed down your metabolism so greatly that any fuel you put in now is burned very slowly. Before you really get involved in your exercise program, you shouldn't expect your body to hop to as it will later on. Also, your system needs this period of adjustment to get back on track. A few pounds of weight gain at this point is not the end of anything—but it can be the beginning of your awareness about food intake and energy expenditure.

Weigh yourself once a week, no more. Daily fluctuations in weight are reflective only of water retention. The only way to get a true picture of your progress is to look at the week you've just gone through. It's best to weigh yourself regularly at the same time of day on the same day of the week.

The Last Drink

Your last liquid-protein drink may be the most difficult. It's like saying goodbye to a friend when you move to another state. Like finally giving up a security blanket. The liquid-protein diet has helped you to complete a project in which you had a great emotional and physical stake—but the project is over.

I would like you to think about making a choice never to go back to fasting. There is absolutely no reason why—after you've learned how to eat, to exercise, to recognize your thresholds of hunger and satiety—you shouldn't be able to maintain the weight you've achieved, and even get below it.

The next key to our program is the exercise plan. In Step II, I'm going to start you on an incredibly easy program that will not only help you with weight maintenance, but will also make you feel better and look better.

Step II. How to Start
Your Exercise Program

Diets are all about food. They mandate what you should always, sometimes, or never put into your mouth, implying that whether you're thin or fat depends completely on how you allow or deny yourself calories.

But diets leave out the most important part of the energy cycle. If you burn energy, you need fuel. Therefore, if you burn more calories, you can increase your intake of calories. This means only one thing—if you want to maintain the

DIGESTIBLES

1. When you're within five or ten pounds of your ideal weight, it's time to taper off from your fast.

2. It's possible that you should weigh 10 or 20 percent more than the estimate for your height and build on the weight tables.

3. Wean yourself back to food gradually, replacing one liquid-protein meal with solid food, as described, every four days.

4. Stick with boring foods that don't stimulate your appetite.

5. Weigh yourself weekly.

extraordinary weight loss you've achieved through fasting, and will now keep off through sensible eating, *you've got to exercise.* There's no way around it.

I can hear the excuses right now: "I always hated gym. I haven't got the time. I can never find a pair of shorts that fit. I get sick at the smell of locker rooms. My fa. 'ly will make fun of me. I can't. I won't."

It may be helpful to go back over your exercise history and see what happened to foil your good intentions before. Ask yourself:

If I am not currently exercising or think I can't start an exercise program I'll stick to, what are my reasons?

Reasons I stopped exercising in the past:

1. _____

2. _____

3. _____

4. _____

Typical of the problems that lead to the downfall of exercise programs are boredom, injuries, failure to chart progress, lack of time, and lack of anticipated results. Another reason many people stop is that they don't get the right backup from their families—who would prefer that the allotted exercise time be spent doing something for them.

Exercise is a tough commitment to make because it means taking a chunk of time out of your day to do something you may never have enjoyed before. But if you've been on a fast for weeks or months and are now at or near your goal weight, you know the value of effort well spent on your body. Since you've come this far, it would be ridiculous to turn back.

Those of you who have already begun a daily activity program will understand what I'm getting at. There are benefits gained through exercise that nothing—up to and including dieting—can match.

- Your flaccid skin and muscles begin to shape up and take on attractive physical tone.
- Exercise reduces your hunger while you're in the middle of it, and, in many cases, for hours after you've stopped.
- Exercise increases your overall sense of well-being and health.

Getting Ready: Mindset

Why don't people comply with exercise programs? Since they're usually aware of how good exercise is for them and how much it's going to do for them, why don't they stick to it over any period of time? Former smokers have better track records; once they've seen the error of their ways, they tend to get extremely self-righteous when they see anyone else veering from the path. Even dieters, though they may fall "off the wagon" every so often, generally blame the particular diet and try another one the following week.

But many of those who drop out of exercise programs, on the other hand, drop out entirely because it's "too much trouble." It may *seem* easier not to exercise; however, sitting around thinking about weight loss certainly isn't going to get you where you want to be—which is on a lifelong mainte-nance program, feeling great and looking great and never having to count a calorie.

Exercise will do all this for you if you give it half an hour a day, five or six days a week. No less.

What does this mean you'll have to give up, in real minutes? It means you may have to read the newspaper faster, or spend less time showering and dressing, or less time obsessing about what you're going to eat and when. On the other hand, you will have more time to think, to play, to make love—because you'll have more energy after beginning a daily ex-ercise program.

Eventually you may develop a real passion for the feeling of working out, and may even build up your duration, your frequency, and your intensity of activity. But forget all that for now. I don't want you to monitor your pulse or count milliliters of oxygen consumed or even get your sweatsuit sweaty. All I want you to do is promise that you'll be active *thirty minutes a day, five or six days a week*.

The Doctor's Okay

If you are coming off a fast, it's a good idea to *see a doctor before you begin any form of mildly strenuous activity*. This is an excellent idea for all beginners, but it is absolutely essential under the following circumstances:

1. If you are over 35 and have never exercised before.
2. If you have a family history of heart disease or hypertension.
3. If you have a personal history of heart, lung, or orthopedic problems.
4. If you have current problems with hypertension, diabetes, high blood fats; or if you smoke cigarettes.

The exam should include a full physical evaluation and possibly a stress test for the heart. Your doctor will know that because you are coming off a fast you are in a particularly vulnerable physical position. Remember, your body is not in a normal state yet, even though you've begun eating some solid foods. Your metabolic rate is at its lowest ever, for the following reasons:

1. You have had a decrease in muscle, which is much more metabolically active than fat. All diets cause you to lose lean tissue, which is why the fasting powder you have been consuming five times a day includes a significant protein supplement—to make up at least in part for what your body is losing.
2. You have a decrease in the caloric cost of exercise due to your loss of weight. Though you might burn 130 calories while running a mile if you are over your ideal weight, you burn only 100 running that same mile when you're at an ideal weight.
3. You have a decrease in the caloric cost of digestion due to less food having been eaten. When you eat less, you need fewer calories to burn the food you've consumed.

With a metabolism this slow, your body is going to take a while to adjust to being active again; only your physician can judge how much activity is safe for you now and how quickly you ought to accelerate it.

After you've been checked out and pronounced fit for action, you should stay in touch with your physician on a regular basis until your exercise program is well established.

There are a few warning signs that will tell you that you may be in trouble. If you have chest pain—especially if it radiates out to the neck, jaw, or arms—or if you're experiencing extreme shortness of breath, you should stop exercising and see a doctor immediately.

Remember that you may experience some "good" pain at first, but this is no cause for panic—or for curtailing your program. You'll probably feel some achiness in the muscles and joints. A warm bath before bedtime will take care of these occasional twinges. You might also consider taking one aspirin *before* exercising, but only for the first two or three weeks of your program, until your body starts getting in condition. Don't get into the habit of taking too much aspirin or other pain relievers; it can be dangerous.

Make a Date with Yourself

The way to start and to stay with an exercise program is to give yourself no option. You *have* to spend that half-hour every day doing something physically active, so make a date with yourself and write it on your calendar—just like a luncheon meeting or a doctor's appointment. If, for unforeseen reasons, you have to break that date, you must reschedule it, preferably later that day or else the next day. And if you've been out of town or particularly busy and have sloughed off for a week or more, remember that you can *always* start your daily program again—it is never too late.

Take the program seriously, and it will pay off. It's just like making a commitment to staying on your fast and drinking your liquid protein for weeks on end—but much more enjoyable.

When are you going to have this date with yourself? You say you're a busy, active person, and your schedule is already overcrowded. Let's try and find a time for you.

Morning Exercise. If you have no real trouble getting up a little earlier, morning exercise is the best option. It lets you start your day on a positive note and gives you the incentive to follow through on healthy activities and compliance with your eating plan throughout the day. You'll be mentally more alert and able to work better. You'll also discover that starting off in the morning with a brisk walk or a session on an exercise bike while you watch a little TV news may help you rev yourself up for the rest of the day. Another advantage is that you can take your daily shower or bath right afterward and lose no time getting dressed and undressed.

Evening Exercise. If your household is simply too frantic in the morning, or if you are a chronic bad-riser, you can select a half-hour in the evening. You might feel less pressured at the end of the day, and prefer to wind down with a walk or with an exercise class at the local health club. You'll have an extra advantage in that exercising suppresses your appetite, which is typically more active in the evening or late at night when many people are lured into snacking. Of course, exercise also revs you up and gives you extra energy, which may be a drawback when you want to fall asleep right afterward.

Midday Exercise. Many firms and corporations have discovered the benefits of encouraging—even insisting—that their employees have a daily hour in the company gym. The fact that big business now recognizes that workers are sharper, healthier, and happier when they're physically active is a remarkable advertisement for getting involved in exercise. If you haven't got the option of taking paid time during the day to change your clothes, exercise, shower, and get dressed, you still might consider using your lunch hour as a time for being active. The benefit here is that you have so much less time to sit around the company dining room, or in front of the bag lunch on your desk, worrying about calories consumed.

An excellent time to exercise, if you are a parent who is at home during the day, might be right before the kids return from school, when the house is quiet and your time is your own.

There are dozens of different options, and you can try out a few to see how they fit into your life style. At the beginning, keep track of your progress with a chart like the one on the next page.

The Family Contract

One the biggest deterrents to exercise programs is not the person on the plan but those who must live with him or her. Spousal and family impatience with, or disapproval of, the time spent exercising is a frequent reason cited by former exercisers for not staying with the program. "My wife insisted that I drive her to the mall that night," or "My kids really wanted me to bake cookies for the fair," are common lame excuses for missing exercise sessions.

There's a very efficient way to deal with this problem, and that's to sign a contract with your family. This contract should be mounted on a bulletin board or kept in a handy location in case it's needed for proof that you've all agreed on a certain daily time period for your exercise regimen.

Here's an example of a contract that's been useful to many exercisers:

Dear Family,
I have learned that to control my weight and enhance my appearance, a program of regular exercise is absolutely essential. I have decided to make a commitment to an exercise program and I am enlisting your support. In order for me to allot this time to my own physical fitness program, you must agree that the time is mine, to be used at my discretion.

	Sunday (day off)	Monday	Tuesday	Wednesday	Thursday	Friday	Saturday
	What I did and for how long.						
	If I didn't keep my date, why not?						
	What options can I give myself next week so I don't miss a day?						

I will be allotting 30 minutes of my time, 5 to 6 days a week, to exercise. I will need an additional 30 minutes to shower and change. I am aware that this might cause some inconveniences for my family, but we are all agreed that we will act together in this very difficult undertaking. I promise to do my best to fulfill my part of the contract to make this positive change in my life; and I ask you to sign this contract agreeing that you will not complain or make any negative comments about my exercise program.

You may take this contract out to remind me—if I have forgotten and missed too many days—that I have a daily obligation to myself to exercise. I may take it out and remind you that you have agreed to support me fully in this endeavor.

YOUR SIGNATURE   SPOUSE   FAMILY MEMBERS

This kind of written reminder is invaluable, particularly when you're just starting. And who knows, it may even inspire your spouse or children to sign up and join you, which is the best alternative of all.

Selecting an Activity

If you have never exercised before, or if it's been a long time since you owned a pair of sneakers, you may prefer to select an activity you can do alone, without others watching you. This might entail following an exercise video that you can play in the privacy of your den, or a session on an exercise machine in your bedroom while you watch TV. Another option, for those who love the great outdoors, is walking.

Remember, it doesn't matter what you do right now, so long as it keeps you active. You don't have to work up a sweat, you don't have to tire yourself out. What you're aiming for is simply getting into a routine that you can't—and don't

wish to—get out of. Let's examine the advantages and dis-
advantages of some beginning exercise programs.

Videos. There's a wide assortment of exercise tapes, in video
stores today, that are graded as to their level of difficulty.
Ask the owner of the store for a tape that will be on your
level. Don't try a tougher one or you'll be frustrated by the
pace and intensity and probably give up before the end. You
can do your half-hour at any time that's convenient for you.

The only drawbacks are that you must own a video machine and have a big enough space to work out in front of
it. You may also get bored with doing the same exercises
each day—in which case you may want to opt for two tapes,
to use alternatively.

Exercise Machines. Again, with this activity you have the
convenience and privacy of your home. You can even com-
bine an exercise session with other regular activities, like
watching TV, listening to music, or reading a book. These
machines frequently have gradated exercise levels that allow
you to adjust the resistance to your level of ability and thus
build up tolerance and fitness gradually.

If you have orthopedic problems or are still carrying a lot
of excess weight, the machines are a good choice because
they force you to work against their resistance, not against
your own body.

The only drawback is the boredom factor, but as you work
into the second stage of the program you can always alternate
your machine sessions with another exercise activity.

Walking. Walking is the most natural exercise you can do,
and has been proven effective for good cardiovascular conditioning as well as general fitness. You can walk anywhere
and everywhere and see the world. You might consider walking to work instead of driving, or to lunch or dinner dates,
thus also saving on gas and parking fees. You'll enjoy a much

lower risk of injury than with most other physical activities. It's harder in bad weather, of course, but the good thing is that you can always change your route and go indoors; many walking clubs have taken over shopping malls before they open in the morning, and there are indoor tracks available at health clubs and other facilities.

I'm not talking about strolling, but about vigorous walking that really gets you moving. You want to stride rather than walk. Instead of moving your feet in two parallel lines, think about keeping your feet on an imaginary straight line in front and in back of you that is powered by the motion of your hips, which should move from front to back, not side to side. Swing your arms and keep them bent at a 90-degree angle for momentum. Aim for a rhythmic gait, one that you can speed up as you get going.

Yoga, Tai Chi, Low-Impact Aerobics, or Jazzercise. If you don't mind exercising with other people, the social factor can be a great incentive to keeping up with an exercise program. First, there's the support of a helpful teacher whose main goal is to encourage you in your exercise goals, and whose expert instruction will keep you from overdoing your efforts or from doing something incorrectly and thus injuring yourself.

Another important aspect of joining a class is the camaraderie. There's a nice warm sense of everyone being in this together—and getting better together. On the other hand, it may be depressing for some to see the more experienced or more svelte members of the class at work.

For beginners, I suggest a gentle class at first. As you move into the second stage of your exercise program, in Step V, you'll be raising the intensity of your activity to get your heartbeat up to its target rate (see p. 97) for complete fitness.

Yoga, an ancient Indian discipline of postures and body movement, encourages full breathing and relaxation. For someone coming off a fast, yoga can be amazingly beneficial in regulating the psyche and giving the practitioner a sense of incredible calm and well-being. Depending on the teacher, it can be static or fluid, slow or fast.

Tai Chi, an ancient Chinese method of self-defense, is practiced by young and old alike in China today. It is a complete but gentle body workout, in which one move flows gracefully into another stressing flexibility, relaxation, and breathing. Like yoga, it is currently offered at Y's and health clubs around the country.

Low-impact aerobics and jazzercise are two forms of exercise offered at most health clubs and are usually performed to music. Depending on the teacher, the activity can be very gentle or relatively stimulating. The class should be small enough so that you can get some individual attention and really learn the exercises properly.

Getting Ready: Equipment

For most exercisers, a good rule to follow is *the simpler the better*. If you don't have to spend a lot of money on equipment and clothing, you'll be more willing to comply with your activity program. Let's start with the simplest:

Walking. All you need is a sweatsuit or a pair of shorts, and, depending on the weather, possibly a set of thermal underwear. It is essential that you purchase a good pair of *walking* shoes, which are different from running shoes in that they have more flexible soles, lower backs, and tend to be a bit less shock-absorbent. A salesman in a sportswear store will be able to direct you to the appropriate ones, which range in price from about thirty to sixty-five dollars.

Videos. Exercise videos can be found for as low as twenty dollars. You should spend another ten to twenty dollars on a padded exercise mat. The only other equipment necessary is a pair of sweats, a leotard or shorts and a T-shirt, and possibly some exercise shoes or sneakers. (The instructor in the tape will probably tell you which shoes to wear or whether you should be barefoot.)

Exercise Machines. You must buy a machine—no small expense. The best can be prohibitive for many people, in the $1,000 to $3,000 range, but these can usually be purchased on a monthly payment plan. Adequate workout machines can be found for about $300. The only other equipment necessary is a set of sweats or shorts, a T-shirt, and a pair of sneakers or exercise shoes.

Types of Machines Available

1. *Stationary bicycles*: New computer-controlled models simulate riding outdoors with "hills" for higher resistance and "flats" with less resistance. Some models allow for interval training, which can help build fitness with less perceived discomfort.
2. *Rowing machines*: These give good cardiovascular workouts. They also build upper body, back, and legs.
3. *Treadmills*: These offer all the advantages of running without any risk of injury. They're also adjustable to different levels of fitness.
4. *Step machines*: These provide a great workout and are particularly good for people with excess weight problems.
5. *Cross-country skiing machines*: These offer an excellent total body workout. They do require good coordination and daily practice. Some beginners may give up because they get exhausted too quickly.

Yoga, Tai Chi, Low-Impact Aerobics, or Jazzercise. You will need to pay a fee for taking a class, or a membership fee in a health club, or both. The classes are generally low cost, but the health club membership can be steep (of course it includes the use of all the club's facilities). You will need a

pair of sweats or shorts, or a leotard, and the instructor will
tell you whether you should work barefoot or in exercise
shoes.

Getting Ready:
Stretching Your Muscles

You should never attempt to launch into your exercise session without warming up. And you should never stop dead
in your tracks—you must cool down afterward. Why is this
so?

If you've ever gotten up suddenly after sitting for a long
time and felt a wave of dizziness overcome you, you'll understand the principle of gradually accustoming the body to
physical change. When you're in an inactive state for some
period of time—sleeping, sitting at a desk or in front of a
television set—your heart is functioning at a rather slow
pace, your blood pressure is low, your lungs are taking shal-
low breaths to ingest just enough oxygen for comfort. Your
muscles and tendons are either slack or tense, depending on
your mood.

When you begin to exercise quickly, you may experience
shortness of breath and nausea; your blood pressure rises
too rapidly, your muscles need time to stretch out, and your
lungs must gradually increase their capacity to consume oxygen.

Warming up and cooling down are essential in both the
prevention of injury and the preparation of the body
for the workout to come. Those who faithfully stretch
before they begin physical activity are much more likely
to stick with the program.

There are many excellent exercise books that give specifics
on warm-ups; but for our purposes here, remember to work
on total body stretches (bent-knee sit-ups and toe-touches,

body swings side-to-side and around in circles), as well as specific muscle and joint stretches (hamstring, calf, ankle, head rolls).

One of the best ways to warm up and cool down is to practice a lower intensity version of the exercise you'll be doing for about five to ten minutes on each end.

Coordination: Exercise Expenditure and Food Intake

At the end of your first week of exercise, sit down and answer the following questions:

1. In general, aside from a few aches and pains, do I feel physically better or worse?
2. Do I feel emotionally better or worse?
3. After my daily exercise sessions, do I feel less or more hungry?
4. If I feel hungry, what am I hungry for? Would it be something more healthful than not?
5. After my daily exercise sessions, am I thirsty? Do I naturally crave a glass of water or of soda?
6. Do I feel more energized? *Less* energized?
7. Do I feel better—more relaxed, more hopeful—about staying on the maintenance program now?
8. On the days when I skipped the exercise session, how did I feel?
9. Do I feel that next week will be easier or harder? Why?

If you're at all discouraged, remember that exercising is a lot more difficult than dieting. It is active work, *doing* something, whereas dieting is passive work, *not* doing something. It does become more enjoyable with time, for these reasons:

- You get better at it and feel less awkward.
- Your body actually shows a difference; your clothes fit better.
- Your tolerance for more prolonged and difficult exercise becomes greater each week, the more you do it.

You may also begin to notice after a few weeks that your craving for certain foods or quantities of food lessens the more you exercise. There seems to be a natural desire for the body to heal itself—and to keep itself healthy. Also, those who did not fast down to their goal weight and want to lose more will find that this combination of elements is a sure winner. Exercise helps to counteract the metabolism-slowing effect of the boring low-calorie diet you're currently on, and thus lets you keep losing weight.

Remember the equation: energy consumed < energy expended = weight loss.

If you are ever in doubt about exercise, or if you've missed four days because of meetings or travel or alarm-clock failure and feel "Oh well, I might as well give up now because it's too much trouble," THINK about what you've already accomplished and what you want for the rest of your life.

For weeks or months when you got up every day you made a conscious decision not to eat solid food. It was incredibly tough, but you stuck with it and persevered and reached your goal. If you can just muster up the same inner strength that kept you on the fast, and use it to make a daily commitment to exercise, you'll find the rewards are even greater than those of weight loss: When you stick with exercise you will feel better, look better, and live longer.

Step III.
Hunger and Satiety—A New
Way to Think About Eating

I remember thinking when I was growing up that one of the dumbest things I ever heard was, "Clean your plate—there are children starving in Europe."

DIGESTIBLES

1. Get a doctor's okay before you begin any exercise program.

2. Make a commitment to exercising half an hour a day, five to six days a week.

3. Warm up before and cool down after each exercise session.

4. Decide whether you want to start your exercise program in the privacy of your home, or whether you need the incentive of a group experience to keep you going.

5. If you slough off for a few days—or even a few weeks—don't despair. You can always start over.

My immediate response—then and now—would be, "What has that got to do with whether I'm hungry or not?"

A child doesn't finish a meal either because he or she doesn't like the food or because enough of it has been eaten. Period. Children eat until they're full and stop right there. But for a variety of reasons, adults forget the simple biological needs that impel us to eat and to cease eating. We tend to eat by the clock because of job or family pressures; we tend to grab food on the run because we "don't have time" to sit down and enjoy it. We tend to overeat on special occasions, because a lot of good food is simply too tempting to pass up.

But our physical needs for food haven't changed a bit since childhood—and now it's time to relearn the right way to eat. Once you've mastered eating when you're hungry and stopping when you're satiated, you'll never have to monitor your food intake again.

Charting Your Hunger

We're going to rate your hunger on a scale that ranges from 0 to 10; 0 represents the feeling of being stuffed and unable to eat another mouthful; 10 means being ravenous, feeling capable of downing an entire turkey with the trimmings and three hot fudge sundaes as a chaser. Look at the following hunger ratings:

| 0 | 2 | 4 | 6 | 8 | 10 |

0 = stuffed, like after a big Thanksgiving meal
2 = full, like after a normal meal
4 = content or neutral, like an hour after a good meal
6 = pretty hungry, like just before lunch after a small breakfast four hours earlier
8 = very hungry, like at 5 P.M. when you've skipped lunch and breakfast
10 = ravenous, the way you felt on the first two or three days of your fast

I want you to think back to before your fast, to a special occasion on which the quality or quantity of food available made you consume more than you really should have. Or perhaps it was an especially happy or sad event in your life. You may have had the same experience that Abby, a typical restrained eater, had last May when she was putting together a family reunion dinner.

She got up that morning realizing that she wouldn't be able to stay on her diet, but it was okay—after all, this was a big celebration and she owed it to herself and her guests not to seem like a spoilsport. She decided to skip breakfast so that when the party started, she wouldn't be as guilty about eating.

She hadn't eaten all night, so she was already hungry—

probably at 7 on her hunger rating scale—but she ignored that; she had a cup of coffee and a few plain crackers at 8 A.M. and waited until noon when she couldn't stand it any longer. She really was ravenous. Her hunger was at the very top of the scale—at 10.

She found a container of leftover macaroni and cheese and polished that off while she made the dip for the party from a fabulous new recipe she'd gotten from her neighbor, a caterer. She ate some of that with crackers as she cooked dinner, just to make sure it was the right consistency. Her hunger level dropped to 6.

There was half of a ham-and-cheese sandwich in the refrigerator, and it was taking up space so she ate that, too, with some of the chips she'd just put in a bowl on the coffee table. Her hunger level went down to a 4 because, for all intents and purposes, she'd consumed as many calories as she would have had in a normal meal. But she didn't *count* it as a meal (she hadn't even put the food on a plate or sat down to eat it), so she still felt as if she needed more to eat. She took a couple of cookies from the cookie jar and poured herself a glass of milk.

Then people started arriving. She had hors d'oeuvres— she can't remember how many—walking around the room talking to the guests, and she stopped back into the kitchen several times to check and taste everything in the pots. She munched on a few cheese sticks, and a few potatoes that had burned and therefore couldn't be put on the platter. Her hunger scale was really at 2, but it was just time to sit down to dinner.

Had she been an unrestrained eater, Abby might have been content with a small piece of meat and a small serving of one vegetable. But as a restrained eater who had already blown her diet, she loaded her plate with the tempting fare —meat, potatoes, two kinds of salad (pasta and green), two vegetables, a roll with butter. It didn't matter, she kept repeating to herself. This was a feast day—tomorrow she'd diet. She had second portions of the meat and salad, and then finally the moment she'd been waiting for arrived. She let Aunt Rose clear the table while she raced back to the kitchen to put together the dessert tray. Triumphantly, she paraded it into the dining room—and she was the first to cut into the cakes and pies that all the relatives had brought. She had one of each selection on the tray, with a scoop of chocolate ice cream to make it go down easier.

At that point, she *had* to know she was at 0. Unless she'd had a stomach like Jack the Giant-Killer, she couldn't possibly have put another bite in her mouth. Actually, she felt awful, as if she had a lead weight in her stomach. But after all, it was a special event.

For many restrained eaters like Abby, being so full of food they're unable to move, or running completely on empty, are the only times they're really aware of their hunger or lack of it. Only 0 or 10 means anything to them because they don't bother to check themselves out when they're in between these two extreme states. On the other hand, most unrestrained eaters don't get themselves to 0 or 10 very often—because they always remain aware of their true stomach hunger, regardless of the circumstances.

There is no reason to eat only when you're ravenous, or to cease eating only when you can't stuff anything else down your gullet. As a matter of fact, *there is no reason to eat anything at all until your hunger rating is over 6. And you should stop when your rating drops to between 2 and 4.*

Mouth Hunger or Stomach Hunger?

Let's examine the above example for a moment. We can say that Abby ate without any regard for the messages sent out by her stomach.

Stomach hunger is felt in the abdominal area, an emptiness or achiness exacerbated by intestinal contractions. The hungrier your stomach is, the more intense the contractions.

When she got up in the morning, her stomach gave her signals that would have indicated it was time to consume food. But Abby ignored the message her stomach was sending out until about noon, when she couldn't stand the pangs anymore. She was also confronted with food that looked and smelled wonderful. When she began consuming food, at about noon, it was with the rationale that this was an "eating day," which gave her the license to "misbehave." When she continued eating, it was because she was in the midst of a social occasion, and everybody was doing it. When she kept eating way past her point of satiety, it was certainly not because she was still hungry.

Mouth hunger is the psychological desire for something to eat. Food is appealing to your senses of taste and of smell, regardless of how hungry your stomach is.

Think about these first weeks of tapering off from your fast. As hunger returns, it sometimes does so with frightening insistence. But when it seems to overcome you, and you've got only one snack or meal remaining for the day, ask yourself: At this moment, would I be just as satisfied with three ounces of boiled chicken and five Brussels sprouts—or would I be satisfied only with a bowlful of salty cheese curls or a wedge of pecan pie? If you answer the question honestly, you'll begin to recognize the difference between *mouth* hunger (satisfied only with the cheese curls and pecan pie) and *stomach* hunger (just as interested in the chicken breast and Brussels sprouts). When you can distinguish which hunger you're really experiencing, you'll begin to eat in a more thoughtful, less obsessive way.

Using the Hunger Scale

For the next seven days, I want you to start relearning true stomach hunger and begin to use it as the primary determinant of whether or not you're going to eat.

Each time you're about to sit down to a meal or a snack,

you will rate your hunger from 0 to 10. *You will eat only if your rating is 6 or above.* If your rating falls below six, wait half an hour and do another assessment. It doesn't matter whether it's mealtime, or whether everyone else in the family is sitting around waiting for you to start the meal, or whether you always, unfailingly, have a little something at this point in the afternoon. For this one week, you're going to ignore every factor except your hunger rating scale. If you're not at 6 or above, *don't eat.*

Remember not to change anything about your exercise program or your meal and snack intake during the first stage of your maintenance program, while you're tapering off from your fast. The food allotments remain the same, and you can plan your menus just as you have been. But during this week you will gauge everything around your hunger scale, which will tell you *when* to eat.

Working on the basis of a hunger scale is undoubtedly going to shift your schedule around. If you exercise in the morning, you probably won't be hungry for hours afterward. This may mean that you have breakfast at ten or eleven o'clock in the morning. (If you are at your office at this time, you must take your food with you and have breakfast when your colleagues are on their morning coffee break.)

If you consume your first meal at ten o'clock, your hunger rating won't come back up to 6 again before three or four in the afternoon, which will be your lunchtime. You might have your first snack at six in the evening, and dinner at eight-thirty or nine-thirty. You might not be hungry for your last snack of the day—it's all right to skip it. Remember, this schedule is just for a week, so that you can feel what true hunger is all about.

After seven days of eating with hunger as the impetus, ask yourself:

1. What does hunger feel like?
2. How is eating because I'm really hungry different from the way I ate in the past?

3. Is it now more possible for me to look at tempting, well-prepared food and turn it down—because I'm not hungry—knowing that I can eat it later, when I am hungry?
4. Am I naturally eating less by paying attention to my hunger rating scale?
5. Does it seem more normal and natural to eat in response to stomach hunger than to mouth hunger?

Once you've gone back to regular mealtimes and progressed to the second stage of the maintenance program, I want you to keep your hunger scale active. You should sit down at the table and figure out how much you really want to eat, based on how hungry you are. Using your ratings, you'll be able to control compulsive snacking and between-meal eating, which tend to be far more culpable for most people in putting on weight than is eating at regular mealtimes.

Before you eat, ask yourself: AM I TRULY #6 HUNGRY? If the answer is yes, eat your allotted food. If the answer is no, do not eat anything at all.

What Is Satiety?

Once you're aware of when you're hungry, you can begin to understand what I mean by becoming aware of when you're full. I don't mean stuffed or overloaded—I mean *satiated*, which is the sensation of comfort, contentment, and satisfaction you feel after eating an appropriate amount of food.

You must know a little physiology for this concept to make any sense. In the brain is an area known as the hypothalamus—the regulator of hunger and satiety. All of us experience *central sensations*, which are mediated by select groups of cells in the hypothalamus. One set of cells controls the sensation of hunger; another controls the sensation of satiety.

Experimental animal research has proven that if you destroy the hunger cells in a rat's brain, he'll grow very thin (since his brain is now unaware of how hungry he is and ignores all signals from his stomach). He may actually starve to death. If his satiety cells are destroyed, he may eat himself into a state of morbid obesity, because his brain no longer has a shut-off mechanism to tell his stomach he's had enough.

We also have *peripheral sensations* of hunger and fullness which are experienced in the stomach and abdomen. The brain and stomach (central and peripheral) sensations seem to act in harmony when it comes to hunger—together they trigger the feeling that we know now as above 6 on our rating scale.

For satiety, however, brain and stomach are not quite in accord. There's a lag of about fifteen minutes between the time when an adequate amount of food has passed into the stomach, and the time the brain records it. The chemical messages traveling from the gut to the brain need that fifteen extra minutes to relay their information. During that quarter of an hour, you will still feel hungry, even though you've eaten enough.

There's another message system in your body that's purely mechanical, which also relays information from stomach to brain while you're eating. This mechanical message travels directly—with no lag time—from stomach to brain, and is mediated by *stretch receptors* in the wall of the stomach.

This message also tells us we're full—as a matter of fact it tells us we're stuffed, all the way to 0. It takes a lot more food to stimulate the stretch receptors in the stomach than it does to notify the satiety center in the brain that it's time to stop eating.

The problem is that if you keep eating, keep ingesting calories because the receptors say you're still hungry, you never find out if enough food had been ingested fifteen minutes earlier.

Restrained eaters get into the unfortunate habit of eating

quickly to end their hunger because they have the awful feeling that they're never going to eat again—at least the foods they most enjoy. Another reason they do this is because they've physically deprived themselves by skipping meals, or by eating too little early in the day, thus mounting up a massive hunger by dinnertime. Then, all they can think about is quelling those immediate hunger pangs. Think about Abby for a minute. Her stomach was full before she ever sat down to the meal, but she didn't stop eating long enough to find out she was satiated. Her stretch receptors allowed her to keep shoveling the food in, which she did unthinkingly, despite the fact that she was really not hungry any longer.

The Half-a-Meal
Satiety Experiment

Now that you can recognize your hunger and know not to eat until you're experiencing it, you're ready for the advanced course. It's harder to learn satiety because of the lag time between your stomach and your brain, but you need this guide in order to figure out when to stop eating. This will help you eat a lot less food each time you sit down at the table—but every bite will be much more enjoyable.

During the second week of Stage 1, at two of your meals, I want you to *stop eating before you normally would.* You will still feel hungry—and you can still have more food, if you decide you want it. But you're going to play a trick on your stretch receptors and make them wait so that your brain can catch up with your stomach.

Take a sample meal. Let's say your lunch menu includes a chicken breast, a slice of whole wheat bread, and an apple. Divide each piece of food in half. Sit down and eat *half* the chicken, *half* the slice of bread, and *half* the apple.

Leave the rest of the meal on your plate and wait fifteen minutes.

During this time, you can walk around the block, fold laundry, balance your checkbook—do anything you like. When the fifteen minutes are up, ask yourself if you're still hungry. If the answer is yes, if your hunger rating is still above 6, finish your meal. If the answer is no, don't eat any more. Remember, you can always have it later—when your rating scale goes above 6 and you know you're really hungry.

See how you feel now; you probably do not feel stuffed, but pleasantly sated. You don't have to make it all or nothing—if you're just a little hungry, you may want to eat *half* of the half that's left on your plate and stop again. By the time you're finished, your brain and stomach will be in harmony again, and you'll understand the concept of satiety.

You're eating less and enjoying it more.

Learning to Pace Yourself

You probably know someone who manages to take twice as much time as you do over a meal. You go to a restaurant and you're reaching for the breadsticks while your friend is busy talking, using her hands animatedly to prove a point. You've already finished your shrimp cocktail and your friend is still dawdling, putting down the fork, taking a bite and chewing slowly, stopping to comment on the excellent quality of the food.

Without necessarily knowing it, this slow eater is naturally pacing herself, giving her brain enough time to catch up with her stomach. Your friend is actually able—without even thinking about it—to experience satiety while there's still food left on the plate.

Some people tend to pace themselves naturally. Others must learn the tricks of the trade. But once you've accustomed yourself to eating slowly, you'll be amazed to discover how much better food really tastes. When you give your brain a chance to respond to taste and texture and the whole experience of sitting down to a lovely meal or a delicious snack, you open up a whole new world of pleasure. And you will have mastered a key concept in long-term weight control.

When you eat slowly, you savor food, you don't gobble it. It tastes better, and it seems like there's more of it. When you pace yourself, you're never stuffed but always satiated.

During your third and final week in Stage 1, I want you to practice the *half-an-hour* experiment. Once a day, make one meal last for thirty minutes. Make sure you have the time to spare and don't have to rush off somewhere. Try to engage at least one family member in your plan so that you'll have company, someone with whom you can talk and while away the time. Lay out your food and keep an eye on the clock.

How can you make a small meal last this long? Here are a few suggestions:

1. Eat one of your courses first, then the second, then the last.
2. Eat with chopsticks—unless you're very skillful with them, in which case you might try a two-pronged lobster fork.
3. Read a book or magazine (if you are alone).
4. Listen to music and pause after each verse, or each movement of the symphony, before you take the next bite.
5. Watch television and stop eating during commercials (unless you're watching *The Tonight Show*—then you'll eat too slowly!).
6. Have a conversation with your dinner partner.
7. Go out to a very crowded restaurant and don't bother the waiter for service.

But you don't really need any devices other than your own good sense, and your diligent attention to when you're feeling hungry and when you're not. Unlike other diet practitioners, I'm not going to suggest that you chew each bite a requisite number of times or eat only in one designated spot or stay away from TV, which might make you slip up and grab more food because you're not paying attention. All of those rules are artificial and unnatural and have nothing to do with learning about hunger and satiety.

When you've embarked on a maintenance program that will be followed for the rest of your life, you can't hide from the daily distractions that go on around you. You can't stick your head in the sand and say you'll never go to a party because it's too big a temptation, or that you'll never eat a bit of chocolate because it might provoke massive uncontrolled chocolate binges.

My aim is to make you a *natural* eater, one who responds to the normal, genetically programmed biological needs of your body. Exercise is helping you to accomplish one physical goal; learning how to eat in an unrestrained way will accomplish yet another. Food is there, and it's to be eaten and enjoyed, whether it's nutritious or just occasional fun for your mouth.

If you know how to eat, you can eat anything. If you know when you're hungry and when you're full, you'll never go hog wild over food.

Exercise to Lower
Your Hunger Rating

There are times when you really do feel hungry even though you've already been through your food allotment for the day. You look in the refrigerator or cupboard and see the wide array of foods that will soon be available to you in Stage 3, and you think, Why not? I'm almost there. And my hunger is over 6.

My advice is to run before you eat. Or jump or pedal or

DIGESTIBLES

1. Never eat anything unless your hunger rating is over 6.

2. Pay attention to the kind of hunger you're feeling. You may be able to stave off cravings for empty calories by eating to satisfy your stomach, not your mouth.

3. Pace yourself. It takes fifteen minutes for your brain to know that your stomach is full.

4. Take time to savor and relish every mouthful. Share the experience of eating with a friend or a family member.

5. Eat less and enjoy it more.

turn on that exercise video. You've already discovered that exercise suppresses your appetite, so take advantage of this helpful physical reaction. A little early-evening workout session when you crave a bowl of chips and a triple-decker club sandwich slathered in mayo can curtail the desire.

I'm not talking about another thirty-minute workout; an abbreviated version half as long will do just fine. This can be particularly helpful if you're going to something like a business dinner or a wedding reception. Before you shower and dress, use your exercise machine or run around the block. You'll find that when you get to your engagement and are faced with platters of food, you'll not only have lowered your hunger rating but you'll be more mentally alert, self-confident, and socially adept. You will have licked the problem before it could ever arise.

STAGE ONE, PROGRESS REPORT

Eating

1. You've decided to stop fasting and start eating normally and naturally.

2. You've set a weight goal that's right for you at this time.

3. You've tapered off from four or five liquid-fast drinks to a complete 1,000–1,400-calorie day of solid but boring foods that won't stimulate your appetite.

4. You've learned that your goal is to become an unrestrained eater.

5. You're weighing yourself weekly, not daily.

Exercise

1. You've made a commitment to exercise daily, which is going to help you expend energy, get your body into good physical condition, and allow you to eat what you like.

2. You have your doctor's okay to exercise.

Moving On

Congratulations! You have just completed the first stage of your maintenance plan. You've been maintaining your weight for three weeks, you've started exercising, and you now understand some of the physiological mechanisms that make you feel hungry or full.

3. You've selected one exercise activity that will get you moving actively, and you'll be practicing it thirty minutes a day, five to six days a week.

4. You've made a contract with your family to help you stay with this daily exercise program.

Body Knowledge

1. You've learned that to become an unrestrained eater, you must eat only when you're hungry and stop when you're satiated.

2. You're using a hunger rating scale to help you decide when it's time to eat.

3. You have practiced eating half-meals, and pacing yourself by eating slowly in order to allow your brain to catch up with your stomach.

4. You're learning to savor food, not gobble it, so that whatever amount you eat is more enjoyable and satisfying.

It's time to move on to the second stage of the *After the Fast* program, during which you will liberalize your diet, increase your exercise potential, and start thinking about your new body and the way you look at yourself.

F O U R

Second Stage—
Weeks Four Through
Eight

Step IV.
What to Eat Now—
The Portion-Controlled
Maintenance Program

Now that you know how to eat, it's time to begin to open up
your options and include more foods in your diet. The basic
principles we'll stick to are very simple, and based on the
assumption that eating is a normal and healthful activity that
maintains life and gives a lot of pleasure. These principles

are extremely easy to remember, once you get the hang of them:

1. Don't count calories. Rather, eat portion-controlled amounts that correspond to your real hunger.
2. Stay on a low-fat, low-sodium diet, going light on proteins and heavy on complex carbohydrates. You should eat no more than three eggs a week, and keep other high cholesterol foods to a minimum. Follow the guidelines of the American Heart Association (see p. 77) and the National Research Council (see p. 83) for general tips on what to eat.
3. Keep track of your progress on a weekly rather than a daily basis.

No More Boring Food

For three weeks now, as you've returned to a solid diet, you've been attempting to keep your appetite under control by making the food you eat as boring as possible—because mouth hunger is proportional to the enticing and stimulating qualities of the food you eat.

It isn't easy, sitting down to something that's bland and tasteless—and it isn't natural. Other than a vine-ripened Jersey tomato, a Vidalia onion from Georgia, a freshly picked ear of Kansas corn, and possibly a perfect piece of tuna belly served as sushi, most food is appreciably better when it's seasoned. The food that you prepare or that you order in a restaurant is usually intended to be dolled up a little.

Unfortunately, the breakneck pace of American life has accustomed us to taking things as they are and buying foods that have already been processed and seasoned. Manufacturers *know* what our tastebuds naturally crave, so they alter many foods before they put them into boxes or cans. For some reason, we are all born with an inherent love of salty, greasy things. And foods that are overdosed with salt or cooked in grease are really terrible for our bodies.

You're going to have to be very careful about reading pack-ages for a while, until you are very sure of yourself as a food consumer. It's astounding how many prepackaged foods are loaded with sodium, which is the element in salt that makes food taste good. Salt is 40 percent sodium and 60 percent chloride, but it's the sodium that retains water in the body and causes tissue swelling and increased blood pressure. According to the National Research Council, your daily intake of sodium should be no more than 2,400 milligrams—less than you'd find in a single can of prepared soup.

FOODS HIGH IN SODIUM
(to be used in moderation)

A-1 Steak Sauce

anchovies

bacon

baking powder

baking soda

barbeque sauce

bologna

bouillon cubes or powder

beef jerky

buttermilk

canned gravy or sauce

canned ravioli or spaghetti

canned stew

canned vegetables

catsup

caviar

celery salt

cheese: regular, processed, and spreads

chili sauce

Chinese food: canned or most restaurant dishes

commercial Italian foods

corned beef

flavored salts (Adolph's, etc.)

frozen breaded fish

frozen breaded meats

frozen TV dinners

garlic salt

gefilte fish

ham: smoked, cured

Hamburger Helper mix

ham hocks

herring

hot dogs

instant cereals

Kitchen Bouquet

knockwurst

kosher meats

"lite" salt

liverwurst

lox

luncheon meats

malted milk

meat extenders

meat tenderizers

MSG (Accent)

nuts, salted

onion salt

party spreads and dips

pickled foods

pickles

pastrami

pepperoni

popcorn, salted

pork substitute (Morningstar)

pot pies

prepared condiments (mustard, horseradish, barbeque sauce)

processed potato products (au gratin potatoes, etc.)

relishes

salad dressings, commercial

salami

salt

salt pork

sardines

sauerkraut

scrapple

sausage

seasoned salts

sea salt

smoked salmon

smoked tongue

snack foods, salted (pretzels, chips, etc.)

soups, canned or dry

soy sauce

stuffing mix

tomato or V-8 juice

Worcestershire sauce

What can you do to make food more appealing to your palate and still remain healthy? Visit the spice section of your market and try out different combinations on foods you love. Be an experimental chef—take an old recipe and adapt it. Here are some general guidelines for flavorings:

FLAVORS TO REPLACE SALT

Meat and Eggs:

Beef	dry mustard, marjoram, nutmeg, onion, sage, thyme, pepper, mushroom, bay leaf, fresh ginger
Chicken	paprika, mushroom, thyme, sage, parsley, dill, cranberry sauce, curry powder
Eggs	pepper, green pepper, mushroom, dry mustard, paprika, curry, jelly (in an omelet)
Fish	dry mustard, paprika, bay leaf, lemon juice, dill, onion
Lamb	mint, garlic, rosemary, curry, broiled pineapple rings
Pork	onion, garlic, sage, apple sauce, spiced apples
Veal	bay leaf, ginger, marjoram, curry, currant jelly, spiced apricot, dill

Vegetables:

Asparagus	lemon juice
Beans, green	marjoram, lemon juice, nutmeg, unsalted French dressing, dill seed
Broccoli	lemon juice, oregano
Cabbage	dill, savory, caraway seed
Carrots	parsley, mint, nutmeg, chives

Cauliflower	nutmeg, poppy seed, paprika, garlic
Corn	green pepper, tomato, chives, onion
Lima beans	minced chives, onion, parsley, marjoram
Peas	mint, mushroom, parsley, onion
Potatoes	parsley, mace, green pepper, onion
Squash	ginger, mace, onion, green pepper, orange juice
Sweet potatoes	glazed with cinnamon or nutmeg; escalloped with apples
Tomatoes	basil, sage, green pepper, onion, oregano

What Is Healthy Eating?

A healthy diet is one that's good for your heart and body. It also happens to be the best kind of diet to stay on if you want to maintain or lose weight. The American Heart Association recommends the following guidelines:

- Total fat in your diet should equal 30 percent of your caloric intake (10 percent saturated fat, the other 20 percent a mixture of polyunsaturated and monosaturated fats).
- Total cholesterol intake should be less than 300 mg. daily.

Saturated Fats
Food products from land animals—i.e., most meat and diary products
Palm and coconut oils

Polyunsaturated Fats
Food products from most vegetable sources
Oils (listed in order from most to least polyunsaturated fats): safflower, soybean, corn, cottonseed, sesame seed (These contain no cholesterol.)

THE FAT CONTENT OF FOODS

Less than 10% fat	Between 10% and 30% fat	Between 30% and 40% fat	Between 40% and 50% fat	50% or more fat
puffed cereal	king crab	pink salmon, canned	ice cream	hot dogs
skim milk	pancakes		Porterhouse steak	avocados
most fruits	scallops	tuna packed in oil	ham	margarine
flake cereal	low-fat yogurt	rump roast	sardines	butter
potatoes	low-fat milk	cheese crackers	part-skim ricotta	spareribs
rice	buttermilk	bran muffin	lean ground beef	nuts
pretzels	mussels	beef gravy	whole milk	sour cream
most vegetables	beef liver	waffles		cream cheese

tuna packed in water	bran cereal	gazpacho	peanut butter
bread	onion soup	flank steak	sausage
beans	popcorn, plain	french fries	heavy cream
Cream of Wheat	pea soup	trout	most hard cheeses
white turkey meat	chicken breast	chicken wings	chocolate
	oatmeal	cheese pizza	potato chips
	oysters	white perch	eggs
	lobster	sirloin steak	bacon
	collard greens	loin lamb chops	mayonnaise
	saltines		
	bluefish		

Food products from aquatic animals:

Tuna, mackerel, and herring are high-fat fishes.

Halibut, cod, and flounder are low-fat fishes.

(Fish also contains Omega-3 oil, which is important in regulating cholesterol. The oil is of proven benefit only in the fish itself—not in capsule form.)

Shellfish are low in fat but contain cholesterol.

Monosaturated Fats

Olive and peanut oils (These contain no cholesterol.)

As it happens, 42 percent of the typical American diet consists of fats; also, the diet has a range of 400–500 mg. of cholesterol. This means that we all have some significant changes to make in our eating habits.

There's mounting evidence that dietary fat is less easily converted to energy and more easily converted to stored fat than are complex carbohydrates or protein. Dietary fat thus offers a greater risk of weight gain, which is why, as you liberalize your eating in Step IV, it's important to keep your fat intake to a minimum.

Avoiding Calorically
Dense Foods

Caloric density refers to the number of calories per unit volume of food. Proteins and carbohydrates (chicken and rice, to use an example of each) have 4.5 calories per gram. Fat contains 9 calories per gram. In other words, one bite of fat has twice the calories of one bite of carbohydrates or protein; this means that any food with a high concentration of fat will necessarily be more calorically dense. How will you know it when you see it? If something is fried, greasy, or creamy, you can probably assume it's calorically dense. Here's a partial list:

whole milk	margarine
chocolate milk	cream cheese
International Coffees	doughnuts
ice cream	most salad dressings
processed meats	mayonnaise
luncheon meats	candy
marbled beef	coconut
hot dogs	cookies
sausage	pastry
bacon	cream
peanut butter	creamed sauces or soups
nuts	snack foods (potato chips,
chocolate	corn chips, cheese curls,
butter	etc.)

For the next four weeks, you're going to avoid all calorically dense foods. In the third stage of our maintenance plan, you'll be incorporating them into your diet, but in a controlled way. This doesn't mean you have to stay away from *all* sweets right now, however. Instead of a chocolate bar—which is sugar suspended in fat—have a lollipop, which is still sweet but less calorically dense.

Choosing Complex Carbohydrates

What's a complex carbohydrate? Bread (especially whole grain), pasta, cereal, fruit, vegetables, rice, and potatoes are all complex carbohydrates. They're more difficult to digest than sugar, which is a simple carbohydrate. The advantage of eating a lot of complex carbohydrates (sometimes referred to as "starch") is that they give you a greater feeling of satiety for a longer period of time. The reason for this is their slow absorption into the digestive tract and the consequently slower elevation of serum glucose. (The reason you feel hungry soon after a breakfast of sugar doughnuts is that when you ingest simple sugars, they are very quickly absorbed and you get a rapid increase in serum glucose—a "sugar rush"—followed by a large secretion of insulin that rapidly lowers serum glucose; this brings on a feeling of hunger again.)

Increasing Dietary Fiber

Fiber, which comes from plant cells, is going to be of great help in your maintenance program. It's indigestible—a good thing, not a bad one. Because the enzymes in your stomach can't break it up, fiber is never absorbed by your body. Instead, it stays in the intestines, either slowing down or speeding up the passage of the other food you've ingested.

Insoluble fiber (found in asparagus, peas, kidney beans, whole-wheat bread, and cereal) keeps you regular by hurrying the food along through your system. *Soluble fiber* (found in oat bran, grapefruit, broccoli, Brussels sprouts, and apples) slows down the movement of food. When properly included in your diet, fiber:

1. prevents constipation.
2. reduces the risk of rectum and colon cancer.
3. lowers blood cholesterol.
4. regulates blood sugars and may lower blood pressure, too.

Americans simply don't eat enough fiber, of either variety. The National Cancer Institute recommends that we consume about 30 grams daily, about twice what we currently eat. But it's not difficult to add fiber to your diet—all you have to do is include in it plenty of fresh produce and whole grains.

Fiber, in the form of oat flakes or rolled oats, can also be used for baking and as a coating for chicken and fish.

Lowering your cholesterol is something you've already been thinking about as you've been tapering off from your fast, and a low-fat diet is one way to do this. But a high-fiber low-fat diet is the best combination of all.

Good, Standard Eating—No Diets

It will be a great relief to you as a former dieter and faster to realize that you never have to be on a diet again. Being "on" means that you can fall "off," and to a person who has always had to struggle to keep weight under control, that fall can seem very far indeed.

What I want you to do is eat sensibly and rationally, and one way to do this is to follow the National Research Council's simple guidelines:

- no more than 6 ounces of meat per day to keep saturated fat and cholesterol to a minimum
- five daily servings (½ cup each) of fruits and/or vegetables
- six daily servings of starches (e.g., 1 slice bread, 1 cup dry cereal, ½ cup hot cereal, ½ bagel, ½ English muffin, etc.)
- dairy intake limited to low-fat products *only*
- daily sodium intake limited (no salt added to foods)

Look at the following sample eating plan, which will probably trigger a few thoughts of your own for menus:

DAILY MEAL PLAN

Breakfast

2	starch	½	cup cereal + I slice toast
I	fruit	½	cup orange juice
I	fat	I	teaspoon margarine
8	ounces milk	8	ounces skim milk

Lunch

2	starch	2	slices bread
2	ounces meat	½	cup tuna, plain water-packed
I	vegetable	½	cup carrots
I	salad		lettuce and tomato, plain
I	fruit	I	apple
I	fat	I	teaspoon mayonnaise
	water		

Dinner

I	starch	½	cup rice
3	ounces meat	3	ounces chicken, baked, no skin
I	vegetable	½	cup broccoli
I	fruit	I	orange
8	ounces milk	8	ounces skim milk
I	fat	I	teaspoon margarine

You don't have to make these guidelines into hard and fast rules to live by—if you get off track for a few days, it really doesn't make any difference in the long run. But if you're given a choice of a ten-ounce burger or linguine with clam sauce, you might opt for the pasta because it's a complex carbohydrate, the sauce is probably cooked in olive oil (monosaturated fat), and clams—while high in cholesterol —are much lower in fat than ground beef. And ten ounces is just too much burger for one serving in addition to being too high in saturated fats and cholesterol.

You don't have to plan meals obsessively. At the beginning, however, when you're opening up to different foods, you may want to write yourself a few shopping and cooking notes that will remind you to stick with the carbohydrates, lower your meat intake, and prepare your food with vegetable oil instead of dairy fat.

Portion Control

We keep talking about ounces of chicken and partial cups of beans and broccoli. How are you supposed to know, offhand, what a reasonable portion looks like? It's hard, when you're cooking for the family and there's always more sitting there on the stove ready for seconds, to understand the concept of one portion per plate.

Portion control is done for you in hospitals, on airplanes (the poor quality tends to overwhelm the good quantity factor here!), and in upscale restaurants where perfect presentation of a ring of cucumbers and radicchio around six delicately poached scallops is supposed to be worth the high price. But there are also more readily available prepared meals that will show you how much or how little of a food is appropriate. For the next seven days, you're going to eat dinners that someone else has correctly portioned out.

Go to the market and purchase seven frozen dietary dinners. Most of them contain about 300 calories, which is equal to the caloric content of the small meals you've been eating as you tapered off from your fast. There's also a very good variety of appetizing frozen dietary meals to choose from—

a nice change from the boring foods of Step I. (Be careful not to buy frozen dinners high in fat or sodium; check the labels. You can purchase "nondietary" meals as well, as long as they are low in calories, fat, and sodium.)

During the fourth week of the program, substitute one frozen dietary dinner for the boring Step I dinner you've been eating for the last three weeks. Keep the rest of your meals and snacks unchanged for this one week.

Diet meals are a great teaching tool for someone who's just learning portion control. Interestingly enough, they are "dietary" not because they omit a lot of high-calorie ingredients, but rather because they are composed of smaller portions than people normally dole out for themselves. Look at the chicken breast on the plate—that's the size you're aiming for. Look at the helping of pasta—it's really just right for one meal. Even the "dietary" pizza can teach you something—it's equivalent to two slices of regular pizza, not the four you might tend to eat if you were out at a pizzeria.

During the fifth through eighth weeks of the program, substitute a frozen dietary lunch for your boring Step I lunch. Continue to eat the portion-controlled dietary dinners during these weeks. For breakfast and snacks, branch out and try more foods.

Make sure you try out a wide assortment of the meals available, and let them be as enticing and stimulating as you please. You don't have to be afraid of eating different flavors and combinations, because now you have three invaluable aids at work in controlling your weight:

1. You've learned to regulate your eating based on true hunger and satiety.
2. You're working on your daily exercise regimen, expending calories as you expend energy.
3. You're controlling the size of your food portions by eating two meals a day that someone else has doled out for you.

Over these next four weeks, you'll begin to increase the intensity of your exercise (see Step V, p. 94). As you do so, stay with the frozen meals for lunch and dinner, but add on an extra portion of protein, carbohydrate, or dairy to bring your caloric intake up to 400 for each meal. This will give you the opportunity to add just a little of your own home cooking and will offer you the challenge of putting together interesting menus.

(If you have a strong objection to eating prepared foods, you may select the Complex Carbohydrate Option. Instead of the frozen meals at lunch and dinner, you will prepare a *two- to three-cup portion of either a rice, pasta, bean, or noodle dish*. This option operates the same way as the frozen meal plan: in Week 4 you will substitute dinner and in Weeks 5–8 you will substitute both dinner and lunch.)

You can now really judge for yourself how much to put on your plate, and you can do it without obsessively weighing and measuring each portion. Think about the boring Step I meals you've had for the past three weeks as you tapered off from the fast. Take that three-ounce piece of chicken and double it to get a reasonable size. Add half a cup or so to the amount of rice or pasta you've been eating. Make sure you can see the china under the food, and you're probably all right.

You'll be eating less and enjoying it more.

But What About the Calories?

Does natural eating really mean that you never have to count a calorie? Yes, but ... You probably won't feel comfortable about the weight maintenance program in Step IV, as you liberalize your eating, unless I tell you how many calories it's safe to eat each day. A rough estimate (which is all you need) is that *it will take 12 calories of intake per pound to maintain your desired body weight.* If you're currently 135 pounds and you want to stay there, you shouldn't be eating any more than 1,620 calories a day or 11,340 per week. If you're currently 185 and you want to stay there, you should ingest no more than 2,160 calories a day or 15,120 per week.

That's a *very* rough estimate, because everyone's metabolism is different. One 135-pounder with a slow metabolism will gain weight eating 1,620 calories a day, while another with a very quick metabolism may actually lose weight. This is why exercise is so vital to our program in terms of lowering your metabolism and allowing you to take in more calories.

It's the weekly figure I want you to consider, not the daily one. Remember our old equations:

Energy consumed < energy expended = weight loss
Energy consumed > energy expended = weight gain
Energy consumed = energy expended = weight maintained

There is no time factor to the maintenance or loss of weight. Weighing yourself or your food on a daily basis doesn't make much sense because your water equilibrium changes over time; and as you exercise, and thus build up lean tissue—which weighs more than adipose or fat tissue—you may actually get a little heavier, though you'll look sleeker and slimmer.

Weekly, Not Daily Intake

The best way to monitor your weight and your intake of calories is on a weekly basis. Thinking in terms of weeks rather than days allows for a much more liberal approach to eating. If you happened to have a rich meal at a dinner party one evening, and you baked a particularly wonderful birthday cake for your son two days later and ate a couple of pieces, that's all right. Really. You'll probably make up the difference on intervening days.

Say you go to a buffet dinner one night and consume close to 3,000 calories in one sitting (and that's a great deal of food!). In the past, you would have considered this caloric lapse a disastrous event, worthy of a new diet and a considerable amount of guilt. But now, think of this occasion as fitting into your maintenance plan. Over a seven-day eating period, it doesn't look so devastating. There are still a lot of calories left to your week (please don't count them—just think about the fact that there are a lot of them). This eliminates all the pressure of having to conform to one set way of eating every single day, day after day.

If you start to think of yourself as an unrestrained eater, you'll realize that this is the functioning pattern of people who never worry about their weight. Let's take the example of Steve, a forty-year-old who's 6'1" and weighs 180 and has been around that weight since he was twenty. There are days when Steve's so active or distracted that he scarcely has time to sit down to a meal. On other days, maybe at a barbeque after the first softball game of the season, he may be ready and willing to down a bucket of shrimp, most of a chicken, and three ears of corn, with an ice cream sundae for dessert. But he never gains weight because he allows his true hunger and the changing circumstances of his entire week to guide his food intake. All these factors balance each other out.

Four Days in the Life of an Unrestrained Eater

Sunday. **Ran 2 miles, gardened,
played ball with kids.**

breakfast: bran muffin and OJ

family dinner: turkey, stuffing, vegetable, apple pie

light supper: omelet and salad

Monday. **Raining, no exercise.
Meetings all day.**

breakfast: applesauce, ½ bagel with cheese

lunch: yogurt at desk

dinner: Home too late for meal, had warmed-up meat loaf and baked potato but didn't finish. Ice pop for dessert.

Tuesday. Ran 2 miles,
showed clients around town (walking),
game of racquetball after work.

breakfast: 2 slices toast, cereal with banana

midmorning meeting: 2 pieces pastry, coffee

lunch (business luncheon): rubber chicken and cold pasta salad (Ate only the pasta.)

dinner: lamb with mint sauce, rice with peas and mushrooms, salad, wine, ice cream and cookies

Wednesday. Ran 3 miles, sat at desk all day,
took bike ride with son after dinner.

breakfast: got up late; just coffee

midmorning snack: 6 jellybeans

lunch: ½ Tuna sandwich and apple juice

dinner: stir-fry vegetables and fish, seltzer

late-night snack: handful of grapes

Here's a person who's eating and exercising more on certain days, less on others. One day's excess calorie consumption is balanced by the next day's calorie expenditure. Another way to think of it is:

Low-Intake Days. At or below the daily level needed to maintain ideal weight.

High-Intake (Liberal) Days. Above that daily level.

Over the course of a week, you should strive for five low-intake days and two liberal ones—but remember, if your balance is off one week, you may even it out the next.

There's another reason I'd like you to forget about counting calories and keeping diet logs. Studies have shown that people experience more hunger on a low-calorie (1,000 to 1,200) diet than they do on a fast. One of the reasons is the awful monotony and hopelessness of getting just so much chicken, fish, fiber, and fruit day in and day out. When you can break up a few low-intake days with a few liberal ones, you have some respite.

Daily maintenance calories: 1,500

Low-intake days	Liberal days
Day 1. 1,000	2. 2,000
3. 1,200	5. 2,500
4. 1,500	
6. 1,300	
7. 1,000	

Weekly Total: 10,500 calories

Shopping Tips

1. Make a shopping list for all staples so you'll have them at home when you need them. (If you have low-fat cooking spray on your list, you'll have it in your pantry and will be less likely to fry food in the butter you happen to have in the refrigerator.)
2. Give yourself leeway on some of the items you're going to buy. You might write, "1 meat, 3 fish, 2 poultry, 2 desserts, a pasta, a new bread choice, a bag of potatoes." The important thing is to shop according to our guidelines—more carbohydrates, fruits, and vegetables; fewer proteins and fats.
3. Don't buy high-fat or high-salt foods—such as potato chips, pretzels, and nuts—in great quantity. If you don't have them around the house, there's less of an opportunity to eat them. When you do buy them, get the individual, portion-controlled packages—not the giant economy-sized ones.
4. Don't shop when you're hungry—have a snack before

you go. It's very easy to be lured by packaging or placement on store shelves.

5. Read package labels carefully. The ingredients are listed from most to least on the side of the box (i.e., if fats or oils are at the top of the list, you'll probably do better to leave the item on the shelf).

6. When buying margarine, be sure that "liquid vegetable oil" is the first ingredient listed.

7. Be careful about processed or prepared foods made with eggs—this means they're high in cholesterol.

8. Stay away from anything with hydrogenated fats and oils—when cooked, these turn into saturated fats.

9. Don't buy anything with coconut or palm oil listed as an ingredient—cookies, and dry cereals geared to children, are particularly pernicious carriers of these oils, which are very high in saturated fats.

10. Enjoy shopping and be creative about it. Don't be afraid to try new things, particularly fresh fruits and vegetables, different kinds of noodles and pasta, a fish you've never seen before. If you've never cooked kohlrabi, but have an interesting recipe for it, give it a whirl.

11. Check out vegetarian, health-food, and American Heart Association cookbooks for appealing recipes that are good for you as well as their targeted readers. There are also some wonderful specialty cookbooks that offer new and different ideas for pasta, greens, fish, and so on.

Healthy Cooking Tips

You can be as scrupulous as you like in purchasing low-fat foods, but you can ruin the whole thing by cooking them in a high-fat medium. Here are a few cooking tips for a healthier diet:

1. Trim all visible fat from meat. Remove skin from poultry.

2. Bake, broil, or roast meats and poultry. Buy a rack for

your roasting pan so that the fat can drip away from the meat.

3. Baste with fruit juice, tomato juice, or wine instead of pan juices.

4. Rub garlic into roasts to bring out natural flavor.

5. Do not "dot with butter." You might try a butter substitute to give the approximate flavor.

6. Don't smear your pot or pan with butter or margarine. Use Pam, a low-fat aerosol cooking spray made from liquid corn oil and lecithin, that keeps food from sticking and lubricates it with a flavor similar to butter.

6. Don't fry fish; bake or broil it or—the healthiest fish-cooking technique of all—*poach* it.

7. Substitute egg whites for whole eggs in recipes. Two egg whites usually equal one whole egg in cooking. (This will not work in baking, but you might decide to bake an angel-food cake that uses twelve egg whites, rather than a traditional cake that uses three whole eggs.)

8. When you have a craving for an omelet, substitute Egg Beaters or Tofutti Egg Watchers. These products, found in the frozen food section of your market, are made from a combination of egg white and soybean; it's almost impossible to tell them from the real item, and they contain no cholesterol and miniscule amounts of fat.

9. Purchase low-fat yogurt, cream cheese, sour cream, and milk. Buy sherbet and popsicles instead of ice cream.

10. Serve vegetables with condiments or lemon juice rather than in cheese or cream sauces.

11. Serve pasta, bean, or rice main dishes every once in a while for variety—these foods don't always have to be just accompaniments to meat.

DIGESTIBLES

1. Don't count calories; eat reasonable portions.

2. Monitor your food intake by the week, not the day.

3. Stick to a high-carbohydrate, low-fat, low-cholesterol, low-salt diet.

4. Allow yourself two liberal eating days for every five low-intake days.

Step V.
Exercise Exchanges—
Resetting Your Setpoint

Now that you have your exercise regimen firmly fixed on your daily calendar, and you've started to reap the benefits of expending more energy and burning more calories, it's time to step up your pace—to really use exercise as a tool to take off those last pounds you wish to lose, and to increase your general level of fitness.

If you were a sedentary person before your fast, and Step II of this program was your first foray into the world of physical exercise, you've probably been walking, working out with a video or on an exercise machine, or taking a beginner-level course at a health club. I want you to continue with these activities in Step V. However, I also want you to accelerate your program now, *and make an exercise exchange every other day for a second exercise activity*.

What Kind of Exercise
Are You Aiming For?

Now that you're familiar with stretching and proper breathing, and you're starting to become aware of your body's potential, you can begin to see the possibilities of getting into excellent physical condition—improving overall fitness and strengthening your cardiovascular system while you continue to work on your weight-maintenance program.

The kind of exercise that helps control weight—that raises your metabolic rate and gets your heart pounding, your lungs expanding, and your sweat glands working—is known as aerobic exercise.

There are many forms of aerobic exercise to choose from, including these:

- fast walking
- jogging
- bicycling (on the road or stationary)
- swimming
- aerobic dance
- racquet sports (tennis, squash, racquetball)
- competitive sports (baseball, football, basketball, hockey, lacrosse)
- martial arts (karate, aikido, judo, Tai Kwon Do)
- exercise machines (rowing, cross-country skiing, treadmill, step machines)
- others, cross-country skiing, dance classes (ballet, modern, tap, or jazz), ice skating

What is *not* aerobic exercise? Anaerobic exercise is any form of activity that is not designed to raise the pulse and breathing rates. Weight lifting, isometrics, and machine-based muscle manipulation (such as on a Nautilus), will strengthen and tone your body but will not assist in weight control.

During the day, you perform many aerobic activities that get you huffing and puffing and raise your heart rate—for example, climbing stairs, sprinting for the bus, cleaning the house—but these activities don't qualify as exercise because they aren't *sustained over time*. What you should be aiming for is to get your heart rate up to training level and keep it there for thirty minutes. This is the *only* way to attain general fitness and help to control your weight.

Reaching Your Training Level

The goal in aerobic exercise is to achieve a specific training level five to six times a week for thirty consecutive minutes each time. This means that, for your age, there is a specific heart rate you should try to reach during exercise that will have these results:

- It will increase the efficiency of your lungs, allowing them to consume more oxygen.
- It will strengthen the strongest muscle in the body—the heart.
- It will allow the heart to pump more blood with each beat, which in turn reduces the number of times it has to beat. The conditioned heart doesn't have to work as hard to recirculate the blood and oxygen in your body.
- It will help build lean muscle tissue and reduce adipose tissue.
- It will help improve your muscle tone.

When you reach your particular target heart rate, you are at a rather high level of perceived exertion. This is a rating provided by exercise specialists that ranges from 6 to 20. A training rate is reached when you feel yourself reaching between 13 and 15.

RATINGS OF PERCEIVED EXERTION (RPE)

6: at rest	13: somewhat hard
7: very, very light	15: hard
9: very light	17: very hard
10: fairly light	19: very, very hard
	20: total exhaustion

Target Heart Rate

What is your target heart rate? Use the following equation:

*220 minus your age = maximum heart rate
(heartbeats per minute)
maximum heart rate × .60 = lowest training rate (13 RPE)
maximum heart rate × .80 = highest training rate (15 RPE)*

You should stay within the training zone of from 60 to 80 percent at all times. Never attempt to reach 100 percent of your training rate. It is very dangerous, particularly if you are a novice exerciser, to push yourself—and your heart— that hard.

The Exercise Exchange

Most exercise programs suggest that you become proficient in just one form of activity. Why then am I insisting that you select at least two complementary ones?

If you develop a passion for running, that's terrific. Running is wonderful for your heart and lungs, and you can actually see muscular development in your thigh and calf muscles over time. But unfortunately, running does nothing for your upper body. And runners frequently run into back, knee, and foot problems. For these reasons swimming, in which you move your body against the resistance of water, is a good counterpart. Rowing, which gets your back, arms, and shoulders working, is another.

The skill developed by one activity actually helps to hone the skill necessary for another. A novice basketball player who has superior aim and a high jump may still be unable to elude his guards. But a basketball player who studies aikido will soon learn that moving quickly isn't always the answer. Aikido, a Japanese form of self-defense, teaches you to be exactly where the other person is not. This could be enormously helpful when you're trying to make a lay-up while being crowded by three members of the opposing team.

You're aiming for total body coordination and fitness, and one sport generally won't deliver all that. A major advantage of mixing and matching exercise programs is that you get to work different sets of muscle groups and are thus less likely to get excessively sore and stiff or to injure yourself. Another advantage is that it provides variety and staves off boredom—the latter being one of the chief reasons that people stop working out. If you think about the fact that Dave Winfield was offered positions with football and basketball teams as well as with the Yankees, you'll see the true benefit of being a Renaissance athlete.

In Step V, you are going to pick two qualitatively different activities—for example, running and swimming, or walking and using a rowing machine, or using an exercise bike and doing aerobic dancing. You'll use them alternately throughout the week for a complete conditioning program:

Running: Monday, Wednesday, Friday
Swimming: Tuesday, Thursday, Saturday

You don't have to be a slave to schedule; for example, if you just happen to feel like running two days in a row, or if it's more convenient, by all means do so. On top of this, if you feel ambitious you might want to include a third alternative, perhaps selecting a sport you've never played—like racquetball or softball—that would offer you a social outlet once in a while. This will add the extra dimension of competition to your exercise program. Sometimes the edge of competition can be a wonderful incentive to become good at something.

Pace Yourself

Exercise, like eating, teaches us a very important lesson: You must learn to pace yourself or you'll drop out before you ever derive any conditioning benefit from what you're doing. It's now going to be more important than ever to *warm up* and *cool down*—first preparing your body for the workout to come, and later allowing it to come back down gradually from its training level.

So far, for the past three weeks, you've been concentrating on *frequency* (exercising five or six days of the week) and *duration* (one thirty-minute period each day). Now we're going to introduce the third element of exercise, which is *intensity*. If you raise the intensity level too quickly, you'll find that it's impossible to keep up the desired duration; in addition, you may become too discouraged to maintain your frequency. This is why it's so important to learn what pacing is all about.

If you are progressing from walking to fast walking or to jogging, for example, you've got to do it in a rational, reasonable way. You can't start out by running the equivalent of a seven-minute mile, or you'd exhaust yourself entirely and never finish the course. But after building from a slow jog to a faster one, you'll find that your heart, lungs, and legs will be able to perform for you toward the middle of your workout when you suddenly put on a burst of steam. And you'll also find that they'll thank you by not stiffening when you come to a complete stop at the end.

You can't start out too quickly or you risk injury and frustration. You can't go too slowly or you won't make any prog-

ress. How do you know what pace is going to keep you at
the proper level? You're going to take your pulse and check
yourself.

If you don't own a watch with a second hand, borrow or
purchase one. Put the first two fingers of your hand on the
side of your neck next to your trachea and you'll feel your
carotid pulse. Count the beats you perceive for ten seconds
by the sweep hand and multiply by six. This is your pulse
rate at rest.

Now go outside and jog down the block, or get on your
exercise bike and ride for five minutes. Take your pulse again.
If you're exceeding 60 percent of the target rate you calcu-
lated before, slow down or stop for a few minutes and then
resume your exercise at a slower pace.

> *If you have never exercised before, for the first two
> weeks of Step V you should aim for a maximum heart
> rate* at *or below the 60 percent training rate. If you have
> exercised before, you can get up to your 70 percent
> training rate—but no higher.*

Remember, the important thing here is to maintain the
frequency and duration of your exercise regimen. Work on
intensity at the proper pace or you'll find your spirit unwilling
and your body too exhausted to continue.

> *During the second two weeks of Step V, beginners should
> accelerate to 70 percent training rate and intermediates
> may proceed to 80 percent. Beginners may accelerate to
> 80 percent in Step VIII—which is as hard as any amateur
> athlete should ever push him- or herself in training.*

The Exercise Regimens

Fast Walking. If your Step II activity was walking, and you've
really enjoyed it, you should stick with it. Walking is some-

thing you can do all your life, and it has the added advantages of allowing you to talk to a partner and enjoy the scenery. If you are walking properly for fitness and for getting your heart rate to target level, however, you won't be talking very much because you're going to be moving at a really fast pace.

There isn't that much difference in cardiovascular terms between walking and jogging. You'll have to walk longer to get the same calorie deficit you'd get from jogging, but it's interesting to note these facts:

- Running a mile in seven minutes burns off only slightly fewer calories than running a mile in six minutes.
- For achieving the long-term benefits of exercise, walking is just as good as running.

Jogging. If you're taking up jogging, you're in good company, because 15 percent of all Americans—30 million people!— jog on a regular basis. Because running is a more vigorous activity than walking, you don't have to do it for as long a time to reach your training heart rate, and you expend more calories per unit of time doing it.

You don't have to run fast, either. You burn almost the same number of calories per unit of distance when running, regardless of the pace. This is why most serious runners are concerned with distance—and over time, as you get more comfortable with your breathing and as your legs get stronger, you'll be able to increase your distance without much trouble. It's better to keep your pace at a comfortable level for your skill so as not to tire yourself too soon. What you're aiming for is jogging for thirty minutes without stopping— but you're going to have to build up to that if you've never done it before.

You should be running on a cushioned surface if possible, either grass or a composite running track. Many running injuries to the legs and knees occur because of the pounding action on a concrete surface.

Your clothing should be comfortable, absorbent and weather-repellent. The shoes you wear should be fitted properly at a sporting-goods shoe department, and you should replace the shock-absorbent inner soles every six to eight months. There are also several very good mail-order companies that will resole and recondition your worn jogging shoes after about a year. Never run on worn-out soles.

The Jog-Walk (Interval Training). For someone who's been doing a brisk two-mile walk each day, this is a logical step up. In this activity, you jog vigorously for 3 minutes, then walk for 1 to 2 minutes. You'll raise your heart rate during the jog, and it will drop during the walk (unless you keep up a very fast pace). The advantage is that if you've never jogged before, this is a less tiring way to approach it. You'll be able to sustain your workout a lot longer and build up your tolerance better than by either walking or jogging alone.

Some sports-medicine experts feel that interval training is just as effective in building fitness and controlling weight as sustained training. It's obviously less stressful to the body, and therefore offers less chance of injury. The *parcours* course, a Swedish innovation, is the best interval training you can get—if you can find one. This is generally a two- to five-mile cross-country run with about ten or fifteen stations where you stop and do specific exercises. The equipment and instructions are waiting for you at each station, sometimes with an instructor to help you out. You can work at a beginning, intermediate, or advanced pace on a parcours.

Racquet and Competitive Sports. The former includes squash, racquetball, and tennis; the latter football, hockey, basketball, and handball. These are all good interval-training aerobic exercises. They offer a great social outlet, and the group pressure to get together every week to play. The competitive edge can push you to a higher training level when you're determined to win, but naturally you need to be reasonably skilled at what you're doing to get your heart rate up to target level.

Racquet and competitive sports can provide an excellent third form of exercise for a particular exercise program. You can be learning a new skill on the court or field while you work hard on your other two activities, and can play whenever the right occasion—and the team or partner—comes along.

Swimming. For the best total body workout, swimming is your sport. It puts no stress on the joints, because all movement is done against water. It can be enjoyed by people of any age in any physical condition and is particularly recommended for those who've had orthopedic injuries. There are currently 10 to 20 million people in this country who swim on a regular basis.

Unless you live in the Sun Belt, you will have to join a pool or swim club, which can be expensive. And if you aren't an expert swimmer, it may be hard for you to get up to your training heart rate and sustain it.

Also, some former fasters may have difficulty with the fact that swimming requires you to wear a bathing suit in public. Although you are now at or near your ideal weight goal, it can still be embarrassing and unpleasant to be around those who have trimmer, more conditioned bodies when you're first coming off a fast.

There's been some recent research suggesting that swimming is not a good choice for those concerned with continued weight loss, because the body's compensatory response to moving in cool water is to increase the amount of fat under the skin. If you are still actively engaged in weight reduction, you might elect to swim only occasionally, using two other forms of exercise as your primary exchanges.

Cycling. There are 75 million cyclers in the country, and many bike clubs that specialize in weekly outings. They also sponsor some fabulous local and international trips. Bicycling is a nonweight-bearing activity, which means that you aren't risking injury by pounding yourself into the ground as you do when running or walking.

But you do need to bike across long uninterrupted distances to get a good workout. You'd have to cycle three miles to get the same benefit you'd achieve from walking one and a half miles or running one mile. Finding a long route, without stop-and-go traffic, may be hard for city-dwellers—and of course, if you ride in heavy traffic, you may be risking serious injury.

You *must* wear a good polystyrene helmet and you should own a five- or ten-speed bike in good condition if you are going to be using bicycling as one of your exercise regimens.

Don't forget, too, the stationary bike we talked about in Step II (see p. 53). All the exercise machines we discussed earlier are engineered to get you up to target heart rate, and you can step up your workouts at your own pace to be sure you're in the 70 to 80 percent range.

Aerobic Dance. Here is a social activity, performed to music, that can be a real mood-elevator for many who've never exercised before. There's a spirit of camaraderie in class—a very positive attitude—and the instructors are generally upbeat, perky people who really have a stake in seeing that you enjoy what you're doing and that you keep on doing it.

It's easy to reach training heart rate with this activity, and with proper instruction you will naturally build up stamina and tolerance. Any gym or health club worth its reputation will monitor you in your first class and put you in a course at the proper level of instruction. It can be a big mistake to start out in an intermediate or advanced class when you're really not ready for it; the results will be frustration, exhaustion, and possible injury.

For self-conscious former fasters who might not be ready

for a class situation with more expert dancers, there are many good videos to work with at home. You should start with a low-impact aerobics tape and work your way up to a more difficult level.

Martial Arts. Though once thought of as the arcane, obscure practice of a few devoted followers, the martial arts have become very popular in this country. Studios where one particular art is practiced, are everywhere, and Y's and health clubs around the country offer additional courses.

Martial arts classes offer a built-in promise of success: the color belts. As you practice more and get better, you are tested by the teacher on the skills you have learned. Passing the test means completing it to the instructor's satisfaction. And when you pass, you are rewarded with a higher-color belt.

Another attraction is that, though the martial arts are very physical—in most cases involving body contact with another partner in the class—they are based on the power of personal spirit. Without trying to seem mystical, they offer a way to think of yourself as accomplished and centered. After all, if you're able to ward off an "attack" in class, it's easy to see how you might persuade yourself to function brilliantly at work or at a party when you feel somewhat shy or inept. Stress management and mind-body coordination are two other important benefits of practicing a martial art.

If you're interested in signing up for martial arts classes, you should shop around and observe several different classes in each discipline. If the students are bullying one another, if the instructor isn't taking control, if the class seems too strictly regimented or too violent, walk away. You'll probably want to try out one of these new pursuits with a six-week mini-course, rather than enrolling in a long program. Extreme frustration is normal at the beginning; extreme pain is not. If you are getting badly hurt, you or the teacher are doing something wrong.

Health Clubs. These have proliferated around this country at a remarkable rate in the past few years. They're accessible to nearly everyone, and offer many benefits for the price. In addition to making available a good variety of classes, they also maintain the most professional exercise machines, with instructors to monitor your progress. They generally have a pool and a sauna room, and a jacuzzi for aching muscles; there are usually a masseur and masseuse on the premises. These places make exercise a sybaritic event rather than a chore—and they offer an excellent social outlet as well.

Other Activities (Dancing, Skating, Cross-Country Skiing). Dance classes and ice-skating or roller-skating, performed to music, can be great for the soul as well as the body if they give you pleasure. There is generally a high degree of perfectionism involved, and dancers are notorious for being fanatical about body image. It may be difficult for a former faster to perform happily in such a situation, but if you can find the right class, and a teacher who doesn't espouse the belief that in order to do well you have to be skinny and talented, these performance activities may serve as a wonderful form of exercise. Soreness at the beginning is to be expected; outright pain means you're performing incorrectly.

Cross-country skiing requires the right terrain and weather conditions. But this is an excellent aerobic activity, and if the opportunity to cross-country ski presents itself, you should certainly give it a try.

Only by experimenting with many forms of activity are you finally going to find the two or three that are right for you. Having a broad base of experience will also let you know what your body is best at, and how it achieves its maximum physical and emotional benefit.

Preventing Injury

You will undoubtedly experience a few aches and pains when you bump up to a higher level of training and take on one or two new activities. This is completely natural and no cause for alarm. Remember, however, that if you experience chest pains or extreme shortness of breath, you must stop exercising immediately and call your physician.

Natural soreness and stiffness respond well to a hot bath or a heating pad; a rubdown, which will increase circulation to the affected areas, may also be helpful. Use your common sense. Skip an exercise session if you're really sore and get back to it the following day. Never overuse an injured ligament or joint—favor it, or do your alternate exercise instead, so you can give it a rest.

To prevent injuries, follow these rules:

1. Always warm up and cool down.
2. Use good equipment—the proper shoes for your sport, the right clothing, a well-conditioned bicycle, a functional rowing machine.
3. Have an expert check your style—if you're at a gym or health club, be sure to ask an instructor to demonstrate a new technique and then watch you perform it. Get a book or a video, and mimic the proper technique along with the expert in the pictures or on the tape.
4. Don't overdo it. Just because you've become a real squash enthusiast doesn't mean you have to play six sets in a row during your second week.
5. Consult a sports-medicine specialist if you have a persistent injury (one that doesn't heal) or if you keep re-injuring the same area.

Monitoring Your Progress

You would never dream of going on a diet without stepping on a scale. Yet many exercisers don't chart their progress in their chosen sport, and thus have no idea how they're really doing. You really do need some objective tracking of your positive achievements, both for incentive to go on and as a reward for what you've done so far.

Throughout Step V and Step VIII—that is, for the first two months you're in training—I want you to keep two charts. The first is a cumulative record of your exercise, like the one on the next page.

Color-code each activity and fill in a block each time you finish one workout session. Pick some goal number of miles or hours of workout that makes sense for you, and plan a reward. You might take yourself to the theater after you've run fifty miles, or buy yourself a new outfit after fifty hours of aerobics.

> For *walking,*   1 block = 2 miles
> *swimming,*   1 block = ½ mile
> *running,*   1 block = 1 mile
> *cycling,*   1 block = 5 miles
> *aerobics,*   1 block = 1 hour

Your second chart will monitor how well you're doing at keeping your target heart rate up during the exercise sessions.

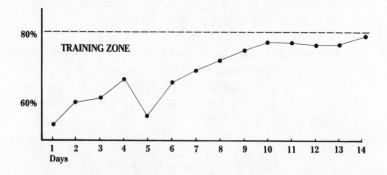

Again, you should reward yourself for every ten consecutive days you spend in the training zone. Of course, exercise is its own reward, in terms of how you feel and look, but it's still nice to pat yourself on the back once in a while and acknowledge your extraordinary new physical achievement. When you can see that line climbing up on your graph, you

TIME AND DISTANCE

Walking (green block)																			
Swimming (red)																			
Running (orange)																			
Aerobics (blue)																			
Cycling (brown)																			

know you're well on your way to becoming an athlete—and to keeping your weight well under control.

Can You Lower Your Setpoint?

Remember the thermostat inside the body that we discussed earlier, the range of weight at which your body seems genetically determined to be most comfortable? If you diet too far below your setpoint and reduce the amount of fat your body has determined is correct for you, your metabolism slows down to compensate and burns fuel less efficiently. There are other compensatory mechanisms working to hold your setpoint to a particular range, such as enzyme production and those central sensations in your brain that regulate hunger and satiety. But exercise, as I've mentioned before, can do a lot to change this troublesome setpoint that makes it so difficult to maintain weight loss. Rigorous activity tends to get all the body's systems working more efficiently, and it also raises the metabolism so that fuel is burned more quickly.

The more you exercise, the more you can eat and not gain weight.

Having started and stuck with your commitment to a daily workout, you already know that your body is in a state of flux—and that this time, it's working for you instead of against you. More than just losing weight, you're achieving a level of physical satisfaction you've never known before. The exercise exchange is a vital and logical step in your progression toward lifelong health and weight control.

DIGESTIBLES

1. It's best to choose two complementary forms of aerobic exercise in order to be a well-rounded athlete and avoid soreness and injury.

2. You should train within the target zone for your age—from 60 to 80 percent of your maximum heart rate.

3. Pace yourself—don't overdo your exercise at the beginning or you'll get discouraged or injured. But don't be timid or lazy and perform at less than your potential, because then you'll never see any progress.

4. Be certain that, whatever exercise regimen you select, you get some good advice on proper technique and equipment.

5. Monitor your progress and reward yourself for goals achieved.

Step VI. The Psychology of Weight Maintenance

So far, the *After the Fast* maintenance program has concentrated on two very concrete forms of weight control—learning how to eat and learning how to exercise. I think you can now see why a reliance on normal, natural eating based on hunger and satiety, and a program of vigorous activity to keep you fit and toned, are helping you to achieve your goal—which is maintaining the extraordinary weight loss you've worked so hard to achieve.

But there is one more facet in our jewel of lifelong weight control that we haven't yet touched; one that is, in many ways, the most important, though also the subtlest and least tangible. That is the way you think about yourself. As a chronic dieter who's failed many times in losing and maintaining weight, you undoubtedly know yourself well enough to admit that you've previously been ruled by certain negative attitudes and beliefs about your body, yourself, and the world in general.

Now that you weigh approximately what you want to weigh, and you're doing some very good things for yourself in terms of how you look and feel, has all that changed?

Maybe yes, but probably no, or not entirely. I would venture to say that you still have some major work to do in terms of changing your mind about how good and valuable you are as a person—and in figuring out whether that has anything to do with the way you look.

How We Learn What
to Believe

It's evident that we aren't born with fixed attitudes about what the human body should look like. Rather, we learn what's desirable and what's frowned on from our families and our culture. As we get older and more independent, we modify our beliefs because of experiences we've had and feelings and ideas that grow from those experiences.

Some beliefs are fluid and readily changed. But others, often the ones we learned at our mother's knee—those beliefs that have been reinforced over and over by life experience and confirmed by others around us—are more firmly rooted. They become deeply embedded in our psyches over time. These are the most difficult beliefs to change.

The beliefs we hold about body image, eating, dieting, and

self-worth fall into that category. If your mother tended to characterize someone she disliked as "that fat pig!" or if she frequently cautioned you that eating sweets would make you "fat and ugly," you couldn't avoid coming to believe that fat was just about the worst physical attribute imaginable. When you saw emaciated models and actresses extolled for their beauty, when the latest diet fad was the hottest topic of every media star on TV, when your sixth-grade teacher told everyone to applaud because she'd just lost ten pounds, what choice did you have? You naturally began to believe that fat was bad and thin was good.

Children learn to view fat as distasteful almost as soon as they learn to talk, and adolescent girls are so obsessed with staying thin that many are willing to starve themselves and risk death by becoming bulimic or anorexic. The real problem with the belief that "fat is ugly" is not so much the corollary that "thin is beautiful," but the adjunct belief that "I'm no good and nobody will love me *unless* I am thin and therefore beautiful." When all your self-worth is tied up in the way you look, you are doomed to failure. When every action you take is designed to make you look better so that people will accept and love you, you're asking for trouble.

Habits That Sabotage Our Good Intentions

We've all got habits that have become ingrained in us over the years. There are good habits, such as brushing our teeth twice a day, and bad ones, such as biting our nails. A habit is an action or thought pattern that begins consciously but becomes almost automatic over time as it's repeated. The more you practice the habit, the more you reinforce it.

Habits of thinking are particularly difficult—but not impossible—to change. Let's say you were a three-pack-a-day smoker early in your life, and lighting up after a meal or when you talked on the phone became something you did almost automatically. Then one day, you heard the Surgeon General's report about how smoking could cause cancer and emphysema. You began reading the warnings on cigarette packs and listening to the TV public service messages about smoking. Slowly but surely, you started coming around. Yes, you'd believed that there was nothing wrong with smoking, but now you knew that you were hurting yourself and possibly shortening your life by doing it. So you changed your belief and broke the habit because you wanted to do something good for yourself and improve your lifestyle.

What about your previous dieting habits? Restricting food, tolerating hunger, then breaking down and consuming large quantities of high-calorie snacks because you couldn't stand depriving yourself one minute longer and anyway, what difference did it make what you ate if you were always going to be fat and ugly anyway? These maladaptive habits and irrational beliefs happen to be the very ones that made successful weight control impossible in the past—and despite your new resolve, and your new body, those habits and beliefs are still lurking, waiting to sabotage your best intentions to eat and exercise in a normal, natural way for the rest of your life.

Two of the most damaging forms of habitual thinking that may have led to your dieting downfalls in the past are your own self-defeating attitudes and negative self-talk. Let's look, for example, at Joyce's situation.

Joyce is a thirty-year-old housewife who, since adolescence, has had a problem with her weight. She's tried every diet from grapefruit to Beverly Hills and no matter how long she sticks with one, she eventually blows it—and hates herself for it. As she looks back and examines her problem, she can remember that there was always some event that—though it had nothing to do with her—made her feel so awful she would start eating and be unable to stop. The last diet ended abruptly when she happened to see her husband eyeing a particularly attractive young woman walking by their house. Let's examine the way her beliefs influenced her actions.

Irrational belief: "I am fat and unattractive."

Activating Event: Husband looks at attractive young woman.

Consequent feeling: Rejection and despair.

Habitual reaction: Blowing diet because it doesn't really matter anyway—"Nothing I could do would make me less fat and unattractive in comparison to that woman."

What was it that threw Joyce off track? It was the belief she lived by—that she was fat and unattractive. No matter how she dieted, no matter how she strove to please her husband, he was always going to find someone else who looked better than she did. Seeing how her husband admired that woman in the street confirmed her old belief, and, consequently, she felt so awful that she lost her resolve to change her behavior in relation to eating.

After Joyce came off her successful liquid-protein fast, she was determined to maintain her new weight and get rid of her old self-defeating attitudes. But how could she change her habitual thinking? Let's do a substitution for her:

New belief: "Men are so brainwashed by Madison Avenue standards of beauty, they can't help gawking at any skinny woman who comes along."

Activating event: Husband looks at attractive young woman.

Consequent feeling: Mild anger at husband.

New behavior: Resolve to stick to weight and exercise maintenance program for her own well-being, not to gain her husband's approval.

Replacing Negative
with Positive Self-Talk

I'm not saying it's easy to overcome your obsession with dieting, your negative self-image, and your self-defeating patterns of behavior. After all, the habits that have made you begin countless diets—and then blow them all—have become ingrained in you over a long period of time and involve some very deeply held beliefs.

But this is a particularly excellent time to modify and change those beliefs because right now, as you look at yourself in a clinical and detached way, you *know* that you're in the process of doing something very good for yourself. This very healthy point in your own development, when you can stand on a scale and actually *see* the extraordinary physical difference in yourself, is an optimal time for creating a positive self-image.

I want you to keep a very open mind and try to explore some of the activating events and false or maladaptive beliefs that continually guide you back to old behavior and thinking patterns. Once you've identified them, you'll be able to start to modify and change them.

There are three valuable techniques I want you to use here and again in Step IX, where one additional technique is added:

1. developing rational, adaptive *counter-beliefs* for every irrational belief
2. working on specific therapeutic *exercises* to overcome the irrational beliefs
3. writing *reminder cards* for your new beliefs, to be posted in strategic places and carried around in purse or pocket.

Correcting False Beliefs

Let's look at some of the most common and deeply held beliefs about body image and weight loss, and attack them one at a time.

Irrational Belief 1. *Losing weight will solve all my problems.* The media wants you to believe that there's something wrong with you if you don't stand 5′7″ and weigh 115 pounds. Why? Because they have a stake in making you dissatisfied with your life so you'll feel that you have to buy a variety of products and services to fix it up and make it perfect. The smiling, beautiful, and thin girl in the commercial is telling you in so many ways that all the happiness she personifies is tied up in the way she looks.

The irrational part of the belief that losing weight will solve all your problems is buying into the notion that thin people are necessarily happier than non-thin people. The maladaptive part is that after you've lost the weight and your life isn't astoundingly better, you begin to realize that you've been set up for major disappointment and frustration. This self-defeating feeling may even make you give up on your maintenance program, because you can see that you're not ever going to reach that unattainable goal.

Exercise

1. Write a list of ten things you anticipated would change for the better after you lost weight.
2. Now put a check next to those things that truly did change for the better.
3. Compare and contrast your previous beliefs with what actually happened.

Undoubtedly, some of the things you anticipated came true and some didn't. Weight loss *did* improve your health and physical well-being. It did make you feel more attractive (but probably not as attractive as you had anticipated). It *did not* necessarily result in success at work, a new romance, or increased admiration, love, and respect from those around you.

Can you identify five problems you need to work on that have nothing to do with your weight? It should be evident to you now that being fat or thin—or maintaining your weight—simply doesn't affect everything in your life.

New Belief: Weight loss can help solve some problems but it is not a panacea or cure and shouldn't cause me to ignore other areas of my life that I need to work on.

Reminder Card.

Now write down five goals that have *nothing to do with weight loss*, but that you'd like to try to reach to make yourself feel you're doing better. These goals should be in clearer focus now that you've lost weight and can see what it actually does and doesn't do for you. I want you to carry your list of goals with you or post them on your mirror as reminders. Keeping track of these non-weight-related goals will help you keep a clearer perspective on those areas in your life outside of weight control, and will allow you to gain self-esteem.

Irrational Belief 2. *There is a perfect or magical solution to my weight problem.* Every time you purchase a new diet book or join a new weight-loss program, you are buying into this belief—one, by the way, which the $15 billion-a-year diet industry just loves. This belief keeps you coming back, time and again, after your previous weight-loss or maintenance program fails.

The *After the Fast* maintenance program, which offers you a sensible way to think, eat, and exercise, is certainly no magical solution to weight control. You've probably discovered by now that this program isn't what you would previously have considered perfect—you may even have gained back a few pounds and be feeling that irrational push toward trying a new plan, something that will get you really skinny this time.

Something like fasting? But now you know that fasting was not a magical solution either. You had to go back to eating solid food at some point. And yet, your irrational belief that something *has* to work may lead you back to the conclusion that you can afford to be less devoted to changing your behavior in a natural, sensible way because if the weight starts creeping up again, you can always go back on your liquid-protein fast for three or four or five more weeks.

I want to strongly caution you against making that choice. It's a very bad idea for two reasons.

First, if you give the rational eating/exercise plan short shrift at this point, you will miss out on reaping its emotional benefits—the new self-esteem you will have by the time you reach Step IX.

Second, if you found giving up solid food difficult the first time around, you will be astonished at how much harder it is the second time. It may be both physically and emotionally impossible for you to tolerate fasting again, and if you recall the facts about body chemistry we discussed in Chapter 1, you will realize that another fast can be extremely detrimental to your health. The more you diet, the more you lower your metabolism, making it increasingly difficult for your body to burn fuel efficiently.

It's far more beneficial to get rid of this irrational belief. If you look at it closely, you'll see its basic flaw. It works on the premise that no matter what you've done to yourself in the past and may be doing to yourself presently, you can always "get fixed." This is akin to the belief that doctors will someday come up with a pill that will cure heart disease so no one will have to bother with lowering their cholesterol or cutting out cigarettes.

The irrational belief that there will someday be a cure for being fat is maladaptive because it serves to make you less responsible for your own actions, less diligent about modifying self-destructive behaviors.

Exercise

Write counters to your old belief.

Old belief: There is a perfect, magical solution to my weight problem.

Counters:

1. The solution to weight control, like most of my other problems, lies in my own efforts and abilities.
2. There may eventually be a magical solution to weight control, but until someone invents it, I'm going to live

by the sound and proven scientific principles of sensible eating and exercise.

3. Life and biology are too complex for simple answers. We may never completely understand the mysteries of the body's and the mind's internal workings.

4. and 5. Fill in your own new beliefs.

Irrational Belief 3. *It's normal to be thin.* "There is a thin person in every one of us, just waiting to get out." This prevalent irrational belief is clearly demonstrated in one particularly appealing television commercial, in which a very thin actress actually jumps out of a large dress, revealing her "real" body.

If it's normal to be thin, then it is abnormal to be fat? What do we mean by "fat" anyway? One culture's "fat" is another's "just right." In the early 1600s, for example, the female form that Peter Paul Rubens painted was the ideal—a lush, fleshy figure that would have tipped the scales at a good 30 percent over the ideal body weight of today's standards.

In order to point up the irrationality of the belief that thinness is normal, let's briefly look at an analogy. Let's say we live in a society where everyone plays the piano. Musical activity is a cultural norm in this society—everyone does it and strives to be good at it. Now let's say that everyone here practices on the piano for two hours a day. Will everyone learn to play equally well? Certainly not—the talent distribution will be extremely variable, with a few people ending up at the high end of the scale, a few at the low end, and most in the middle, as average players. We can illustrate this pattern in the population as a bell-shaped curve.

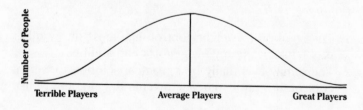

What are the variables that decide which category people will fall into, given the same amount of daily practice?

1. Genetic factors, like a sense of rhythm, a good ear, and nimble fingers.
2. Early environmental factors, such as positive reinforcement in the home and exposure to music on a daily basis.
3. Behavioral factors, such as intensity and concentration during practice sessions.

Now let's examine a belief that will lead us back to our original question about body weight:

In our piano-playing society, it's *normal* to be a
_____ piano player.

a. Good,   b. Bad,   c. Average.

The question *has no answer.* There are simply too many variables. There is no normal player, only individual players whose talents reflect their unique combinations of genetic, early environmental, and behavioral characteristics. Even if you change one of the factors—the behavioral—and have an "average" player increase his practice time to eight hours a day, it might not make a significant difference. There is an upper limit to how good someone can get, no matter how hard he tries.

If you can accept this line of reasoning, you'll begin to understand why the belief "It's normal to be thin" is irrational and maladaptive. As it happens, we don't live in a society where we're expected to be great piano players—so our self-worth isn't tied up in how talented or untalented we happen to be. We may even be able to joke about our tin ears or inability to stay on key.

We don't seem to be able to accept our weight with the same equanimity, however, and the reason is that our society *rewards and idealizes* the thin people and tends to *ignore and look down on* the heavier ones. This means that we get

very competitive when it comes to body image—dieting as
if we were practicing that piano eight hours a day, trying our
utmost to get better. But weight, as we know, isn't subject
only to environmental or behavioral factors. It's greatly determined by the individual's setpoint—a *genetic* variable that's
very difficult to alter.

Now let's go back a minute to the question of what we
mean by fat and thin. Like the talent of the piano players,
our body weights tend to be distributed on a bell-shaped
curve. Most body weights cluster around the middle with
increasingly smaller numbers clustering toward the ends.

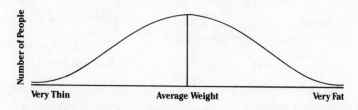

Where would you place yourself on this curve? An amazing
75 percent of 33,000 readers polled by *Glamour* magazine in
1984 reported that they felt they were "too fat." In truth, only
25 percent of them were above ideal body weight. If you
personally believe that you are too fat, you are falling for
the message being delivered by the fashion industry, TV, the
movies, and Madison Avenue (whose models range in the
lowest 5–15 percent of that bell-shaped curve—the message
that if you are not very thin, *you are, by default, fat.*

The ideal weight standards set by the media look like this:

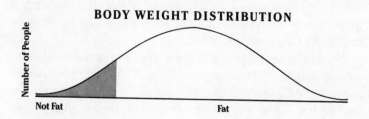

If you go by media standards, you are not thin if you happen to be over that 15% cutoff. And by extension, if that is thin and thin is normal, then fat is abnormal.

But wait a minute. Suppose you've just reached the ideal weight for your height on the table. Suppose your friend, who is five pounds *below* her ideal weight, doesn't happen to be under that fashionable 15 percent cutoff. But you consider her thin! She, however, thinks she's fat. She's not making up her disgust with her body image—she really believes it. And according to the standards by which she's judging herself, she's correct.

It's not just a question of a weight on a scale, either. You may consider yourself fat if you have wide hips, large breasts, or sagging buttocks. Even a few cellulite bumps on your thighs may make you rage against the heavens.

How can you change your belief that if you aren't thin by society's standards, then you are necessarily fat, and that by being "fat" you are abnormal? By making two logical comparisons.

Exercise

1. Get a piece of paper and divide it into two vertical columns. Divide these horizontally and label them as follows:

	Skinnier Than Me	Heavier Than Me
Magazine Ads		
Real World		

2. Women should examine the first set of criteria by looking at a women's magazine; men by looking at a men's magazine. Starting on page 1, put a check in the appropriate column for the first hundred models appearing in the ads and articles. You'll note that all or nearly all

the check marks will be in the "skinner than me" column.

3. Now take your chart to a shopping mall or a busy street. Put a check mark in the appropriate column for the first hundred people of your sex walking by who roughly correspond to your age. Try your best to be an impartial judge, or have a friend or family member beside you for assistance. You may be startled to see the number of check marks in the "heavier than me" column based on this real-world poll.

4. Take these informal polls frequently to reinforce your new appreciation of where you stand in relation to others in the real world.

New Belief

The only reason I feel fat is because I am judging myself by "magazine" standards, not by the bell-shaped distribution of body weights in the real world. It isn't "normal" to be "thin" or "fat"—it is simply our designation of what we think of as thin or fat that makes a difference to us. If I can change my opinion of what "fat" is, I'll be much more contented with myself.

Irrational Belief 4. *Compulsive eating is an emotional disorder.* It may be very appealing to you to believe that you can't control your weight because you have some sort of sickness that forces you to eat. When you're sick, you can't possibly be culpable. Your late-night binges, your propensity for blowing any diet you put yourself on, your inability to control your food intake, are the result of a compulsion—a kind of food-addiction that has a life and purpose of its own.

Part of this irrational belief is that the compulsive eater eats to counteract feelings of loneliness, boredom, anger, frustration, and fatigue. The "sick" eater has a "disease" that only goes into temporary remission during a diet. As soon as the diet is broken, the compulsion again rears up in full force to destroy all the sufferer's efforts to keep weight off.

The only apparent solution or cure is to remove the of-fending agent—the "drug" of the compulsive eater—tasty food. People who think of themselves as binge-eaters don't have a craving for broccoli and oat bran, of course. They want the "bad" foods—sugar and fat-filled snacks. Experi-ments have shown that nearly all people have a biological urge for greasy and sweet foods, and for a binge-eater these tend to be the only foods that will fill the void of depression and anxiety. They also happen to be the ones that will cause the quickest weight gain. So, the theory runs, if you don't keep in the house the foods you tend to gorge yourself on, the eating can't go out of control. Out of sight, out of mouth. But not, I must point up, out of mind.

Now let's get rid of this irrational belief. Take a cold, hard look at this "compulsive" eater. What is she but a typical restrained eater who feels she's never going to let herself have these foods again? Since she's decided to start a new diet tomorrow, she might as well indulge herself now.

There's no such thing as compulsive eating, only restrained eating on the down side of its cycle. As long as you cling to the maladaptive belief that there are foods or situations that will stimulate an uncontrollable eating binge, you'll never be an unrestrained eater and will always be clinging to a rem-nant of the dieting mentality you used to have.

The habitual patterns of restrained eaters—struggling up to the top of the dieting mountain and then slipping down as they blow it, restricting food intake, tolerating hunger, foregoing exercise—demonstrate a kind of self-defeating thinking. This is something you simply must break out of. In Chapter 5, you're going to learn how to eat all the forbidden "trigger" foods that have previously caused you so much anxiety. But right now, we're going to work on the irrational belief that compulsive eating is an emotional disorder.

Exercise 1

You are going to prove to yourself that reaching for food when you're tired, bored, or frustrated is not an uncontrollable drive but rather a habitual behavior that can be changed with practice and effort.

1. You are going to use a technique called "STOPPING." What I want you to do when you find yourself reaching for high-calorie snacks is to interrupt this almost automatic behavior by yelling "*STOP!*" as loud as you can. (This may seem embarrassing at first, and you may want to warn your family if you expect some hassling, but it's a proven, effective technique and will work for you if you do it consistently.)

   If you're having problems yelling out loud, you may shout the word *STOP* silently to yourself. As long as you are firmly telling yourself to end this self-defeating behavior, you're going to be able to learn a more positive way of dealing with frustration and anxiety.

2. Now you must replace reaching for food with a substitute activity. When you experience boredom, depression, fatigue, anxiety, or another feeling that's stimulated your desire to eat in the past, begin another non-food-related activity that means something to you and gives you pleasure. For example:

   • Call a friend.
   • Take a warm bath.
   • Take a slow, leisurely walk.
   • Give yourself a brief exercise session.
   • Read a book.
   • Start a jigsaw puzzle.
   • Play a computer game.
   • Start practicing the instrument you used to play in high school.
   • Go down to your basement workshop and start building something.
   • FILL IN, AS YOU PLEASE, WITH YOUR OWN FAVORITES.

Some activities you select may be fun, restful, or temporarily fulfilling. Others can build toward long-term projects and goals. It doesn't matter what it is as long as it's an adequate substitute for eating. As soon as you see that you can be relaxed and distracted while doing something else, you'll begin to understand that you are not compulsively driven by forces outside your control.

Exercise 2

1. Keep a diary to track your progress. Each night, just before bed, take a few minutes to write down anything positive you did during the day to counteract any feelings you might have had of boredom, depression, frustration, and/or anxiety. You should take particular note of activities you specifically planned as substitutes for eating.

Feeling	Time	Activity
Angry	Noon	Went for walk
Tired	8 P.M.	Called Judy
Depressed	10 P.M.	Played Nintendo

Keep your diary very simple; it is just a reminder to yourself that you have been changing your behavior with relation to eating and that you can continue to change it.

New Habits for Old

The amazing thing about the human psyche is that it remains resilient and adaptable regardless of all the pressures, the difficulties, and the disappointments of modern life. It's only hard to get out of ruts when you say *I can't, I'm stuck, I'm here forever.* The minute you realize that over the years you've gotten yourself out of countless bad habits, self-destructive patterns, and unfortunate situations, you'll be

STAGE TWO, PROGRESS REPORT

Eating

1. You're not counting calories; instead, you're eating three portion-controlled meals daily.

2. Your diet is low in fat, sodium, and cholesterol, and high in carbohydrates and fiber.

3. You're avoiding calorically dense foods, which have up to twice as many calories per bite as other foods.

4. You're eating two frozen dietary dinners or two- to three-cup servings from the complex carbohydrate option to give you a good idea of appropriate portions.

5. You have five low-intake and two liberal days per week, making up your *weekly* maintenance plan.

Exercise

1. You're exchanging one form of aerobic exercise for another while exercising five or six days a week, thirty minutes a day, to achieve total body coordination and fitness and to avoid injury.

2. Your goal is to raise your metabolism and lower your setpoint by expending more energy and burning more calories.

able to see that it's not so hard to change—as long as you want to.

At the beginning, the emotional component of weight maintenance will probably be more resistant to change than the physical. It's one thing to eat the right foods and set aside a

3. You're reaching your training level by working toward either 13–15 RPE or 60 to 80% of a maximum heart rate of 220 minus your age.

4. You're pacing yourself, not overdoing or underdoing your exercise.

5. You're charting your progress daily.

Body Knowledge

1. You realize that even though you're getting thinner and fitter, you still hold some old, negative beliefs about body image.

2. You're trying to replace old maladaptive habits and beliefs with positive counter-beliefs.

3. You're doing exercises and writing yourself reminders designed to point up more rational ways of looking at yourself and those others to whom you compare yourself.

4. You're starting to realize that your weight is not the source of all your problems or your self-worth.

time for exercise; but it's a more difficult thing to tell yourself that you're basically a fine person whatever you weigh, if this is something you never believed before.

However, as you become more proficient in recognizing your hunger and satiety, and as you improve your body and spirit with exercise, you're going to start feeling there's nothing you can't do. Change your habitual thinking, change your mood, in the same pragmatic way that you've already changed your eating and activity programs, and you'll be a far more contented person. Not a perfect person, just better able to live with yourself.

DIGESTIBLES

1. Habits of thinking are probably more difficult to change than habits of eating and exercising because they're harder to identify.

2. Habits are learned behavior; they can be unlearned, and new, more positive habits can take their place.

3. If you can replace negative, self-defeating thoughts with rational beliefs about body image and weight control, you're more than halfway toward your maintenance goals.

4. By substituting rational, adaptive beliefs about yourself for irrational, maladaptive ones, it will be far easier to keep up a normal, natural program of eating and exercising.

5. Writing down counter-beliefs, and practicing exercises to reinforce new learning about self-worth and body image, will help to keep you from slipping back into old, habitual patterns.

Final Stage—Week Nine Through the Rest of Your Life

Step VII.
No Forbidden Foods—
How to Eat for the Rest
of Your Life Without
Counting Calories

As a former faster who knows all the intimate secrets of your body and mind, you are undoubtedly amazed at the changes that have taken place in you over these few short months. Things that you never thought possible are now, through your own perseverance and diligence, right within your grasp.

You've changed your lifestyle—you eat and exercise sensibly, and you have a better estimation of your own worth.

This does not mean that you are a different person. Things you enjoyed before are still enjoyable—why shouldn't they be? You can't go through the rest of your life craving only carrot sticks and a forty-mile bike ride. Sometimes, after a hard day at the office or a vigorous afternoon pumping away at your exercise machine, only a candy bar will do.

No Forbidden Foods—Really!

A ... what? *What* did he say? Candy bar? Aren't those dirty words? Didn't you resolve when you began your fast that you would never, under any circumstances, touch chocolate to your lips again?

I want to tell you that that is an impossible resolve. There is no reason in the world why you should fear or avoid *any* food. Now that you know how to eat and how to exercise, you can eat anything. Because in order to become a true unrestrained eater, who is able to regulate intake by using an awareness of real hunger and real satiety—you must be able to sample and savor all foods, from an ice-cream sundae with hot fudge to a Big Mac with fries. Whatever you want is perfectly all right in moderation. Yes, really.

Trigger-Food Avoidance

Many chronic dieters have had it drummed into them that there are certain forbidden or "trigger" foods they must not eat because one brush of them against the tongue would unleash a terrible binge, which would, of course, mean ingesting hundreds of thousands of fat-producing calories.

Many post-fasting maintenance programs advise making a list of your particular albatrosses and banishing them forever from your home and your life. According to this advice, if you are particularly attracted to potato chips and you know you can't eat just one, you must never even consider them.

If you have a thing for fudge, forget about it because now, as far as you're concerned, it doesn't exist.

The forbidden-food idea makes sense only if you accept the fact that there is such a thing as a compulsive eater—but in the last chapter I showed you that the notion of compulsive eating is a fallacy. The only thing that "makes" people unable to stop eating is their dieting mentality. It's the restrained eater desperate to cram every morsel of this fabulous food into his mouth because he knows he can never have it again.

But if you've ever been in this situation—and I'm sure you have—you know that you still want it and can't help craving it. And it's this irrational dieting concept that keeps alive the risk that you will lose control and gain back weight. If, instead, you accept the fact that you can eat anything, at any time, you will be able to learn that a reasonable portion of a cannoli or a small slice of coconut custard pie will not kill you or cause you to put on an extra pound. As a matter of fact, you'll be able to have another portion of something wonderful a little later, or tomorrow. And that reasonable and sane portion will probably be enough to satiate the most demanding palate.

Why Sweets Have Such a Bad Reputation

There is no society in which people do not indulge in sticky, syrupy, sugary treats. It starts right after birth when the newborn baby is handsomely rewarded for sucking by getting the sweet taste of its mother's milk. All people—not just fat ones—crave sweets. Mankind has had a sweet tooth throughout recorded history. But today, because of the increased availability and variety of foods, we're consuming more sweets than ever—and often more than we're even aware of. Sugar is put into almost every prepared food we buy, from cereal to catsup. Just try to find a package on your supermarket shelf that doesn't have sugar listed as one of the ingredients!

Well, what's so bad about sugar? After all, it's the most frequently mentioned of all the forbidden foods. *Why* are you supposed to restrict its intake if you want to control your weight?

Sugar is a carbohydrate, which means that it contains 4.5 calories per gram, just like bread or pasta. What distinguishes sugar from the two "healthy" foods I just mentioned is that it is a *simple* rather than a *complex* carbohydrate. It's composed of only one or two of the sugar molecules (simple monosaccharides or disaccharides), as opposed to the long chain of sugar molecules which make up complex carbohydrates.

All sugars are basically the same. Whether we're talking about white sugar, brown sugar, honey, molasses, or fruit sugar, they're all basically empty calories, and their only bonus is that they supply quick energy to the body. They have little or no vitamins or nutrients or any of the other building blocks the body uses for daily maintenance and growth. If you're eating too much sugar on a regular basis, then too many of the calories you're ingesting are wasted— they contribute nothing to the nutritional good of your body. You can see how unbalanced you'd be if 800 of your daily 1,500 calories were squandered on sugar, leaving only 700 calories for nutritional foods.

Sugar has a bad reputation not only because it provides empty calories, but because of the way it's usually prepared and served. Human beings really seem to crave sugar suspended in fat—a moist texture, rather than a dry or wet one. After all, what could be more tempting than cream filling between two chocolate wafers (Oreos) or ice cream spooned liberally on birthday cake?

Fats are the most calorically dense of all foods, and sugar is frequently combined with fat. If you recall our discussion in Step V of caloric density, you'll remember that fats pack a real wallop calorically—they contain 9 calories per gram as opposed to 4.5.

Another reason for sugar's terrible reputation is its contribution to dental caries (cavities) and hypoglycemia. Let's look at both of these problems.

Why does sugar cause cavities? If sugar remains in the mouth after ingestion, it feeds the bacteria that can erode tooth tissue. But if you get rid of the sugar, by brushing or even rinsing, you won't be severely at risk for cavities. Sticky sweets—even the "healthy" ones like raisins—are dangerous to your teeth because they're hard to remove. If you eat them between meals as snacks, it's worse than if you enjoyed them as dessert, after a meal. When you consume a meal and have sweets with it, the action of the other food in your mouth offsets the effect of the sugar. The best prevention is the best cure—if you brush and floss daily, you'll help to prevent the formation of cavities.

Now let's examine the other frequently discussed reason not to eat sweets. Sugar has frequently been connected to emotional problems, a state known as reactive hypoglycemia, more informally known as "the sugar blues." The theory is that ingestion of concentrated sweets can be emotionally devastating, frequently leading to nervousness, irritability, inability to concentrate, malaise, and depression. The reality is that reactive hypoglycemia is a rare physical condition— the incidence is about one tenth to one twentieth that of diabetes, but it is frequently overdiagnosed.

Physicians sometimes find it easy to treat a diffuse group of emotional symptoms by explaining them away physically—and "magically"—as low blood sugar. But just putting depressed, anxious people on six small complex-carbohydrate meals a day (the traditional treatment for hypoglycemia) and restricting all simple sugars, will not necessarily cause the "blues" to go away—they won't if the person doesn't suffer from low blood sugar but has symptoms that are psychogenic in origin.

Just because a person suffers from anxiety, depression, or fatigue doesn't necessarily mean that he can't process sugar.

The only way to diagnose this illness is by having a reputable physician draw a blood level of glucose when the patient is symptomatic and have it tested for low blood sugar in a laboratory.

Are there any people who *must* restrict sugars? Yes— everyone suffering from diabetes should follow their physicians' nutritional advice and strictly monitor their intake of sweets.

The Benefits of Hard Candy

Sugar actually isn't extremely fattening. It's only 15 calories a teaspoon, and in and of itself it doesn't hold that much allure for someone with a sweet tooth. After all, who has binges on table sugar? A piece of hard candy, which is just hardened sugar, is nowhere near as calorically dense as a chocolate bar—the dually disastrous fat-and-sugar combination.

CALORIE CONTENT OF CANDY

Candy Bars (Sugar Plus Fat)		Hard Candy (Sugar)	
6 Hershey's Kisses	150	Tootsie Roll Pop	55
Heath Bar	140	Root Beer Barrel (1)	39
Kit Kat	210	Jawbreakers (1)	8
1 Small Package M&M's (plain)	235	Life Savers (1)	10
		Life Savers Lollipop	45
Mars Bar	255	Long-Lasting (one hour) Lollipop	100
Milky Way	270		
Mounds Bar	230	Breath Savers (Certs)	8
Almond Joy	220	Cough Drops (Smith Bros.)	8
Three Musketeers	280		

When you have a craving for sweets, have a hard candy. Keep a bag around the house, and if you feel the urge, go right ahead. A large lollipop costs you only 100 calories— exactly as much as an apple!—and it will last you up to an hour.

The Dessert Connection

Because of a complex physiological process, a "glucose load" (that's a dose of concentrated sweets of any variety) may be necessary to some people to fully stimulate the cells in the brain's satiety center. What actually happens is that the glucose rushing into the blood encourages the pancreas to secrete insulin, a hormone that helps certain amino acids cross into the brain. One of these amino acids, tryptophan, triggers the production of a certain chemical in the brain known as serotonin; this chemical stimulates the satiety center, giving a feeling of total satisfaction after a meal. As an extra bonus, serotonin also helps relieve feelings of tension.

So eating dessert can actually help you to eat less. Because you feel good *and* you feel satiated (due to the serotonin), you don't need to continue eating.

To find out if you need to make a "dessert connection," try the satiety exercise (see Step III, p. 65) once *with* a sweet and once *without*—two Hershey's Kisses (50 calories) or the equivalent is as much as I want you to have right now. Is there a difference in the way you feel? If so, you will need to include dessert in your meal to be fully satisfied.

After a meal, then, if dessert is to be two chocolate Kisses, first eat one Kiss; wait five minutes, then eat the second. You'll discover that you've satisfied your desire for a sweet and now feel satiated from the total amount of food you've consumed during your whole meal.

Don't worry about unleashing a binge. Because you feel full, you won't feel as great a need for between-meal snacks. You will be eating less and enjoying more of the things that satisfy your mouth hunger.

A reasonable portion of sweets is not going to tip your weekly calorie maintenance plan, nor will it tip the scales. At first, you might eat a little bit too much of what tastes good to you. But when you correct your course by checking your hunger and satiety level, you'll find that less will suffice.

Keep the foods you crave—in portion-controlled amounts, if possible—readily available in the house. This may sound scary, but it's the only way you can show yourself that you can handle these foods.

Bites

The most important concept you can learn to help liberalize your eating is what I call *bites*.

If you can think about eating bite-sized portions of calorically dense foods to satisfy your mouth hunger, you will never have to worry about killing yourself with calories and loading on extra pounds.

For the next two weeks, you will introduce calorically dense foods into your daily eating. You'll stop eating after you've had five bites of any particular sweet or snack food.

Initially, I want you to delay experimenting with any fried or fast food (we'll get to those in a moment), but just to concentrate on desserts, candy, and snack foods such as chips. You may have *five bites* of any previously forbidden food you elect to eat at any one time. Five, and that's all. That will be enough to take care of the mouth hunger and satisfy your desire for one particular kind of food.

You can probably see that this exercise will help you differentiate between stomach and mouth hunger. If you're still hungry after five bites of a doughnut or an ice-cream cone, you shouldn't treat that hunger with calorically dense food. You should treat it with something else that's going to get you to your satiety level, like fruit (also high in sugar).

This is not to say that you will have to go through the rest of your life stopping at five bites of calorically dense foods. But by restricting your intake for the next two weeks, you will prove to yourself that you can satisfy your urges for sweets and snacks with a lot fewer calories than you used to.

Tips on Sweets and Snacks

1. Buy your snacks in small bags. Chips come in individually wrapped portions, usually just enough to cover a quarter of your plate, next to your sandwich.
2. Buy salt-free chips, crackers, and nuts. Once you start eating them on a regular basis, you won't miss the salt.
3. Buy candy bars in small or bite-sized pieces. (The small ones are about 150 to 200 calories less than the big ones.) Put the rest in the freezer—they take longer to eat when they're frozen. Speaking of frozen food, you may be happy to learn that even the delicious, calorically dense DoveBar is available in a bite-sized form called a Rondo.

What to Do About Fatty Foods

The other traditionally forbidden food category is fat. Fatty foods include fast food, fried food, fried snacks (potato chips, cheese curls, corn chips, and nuts,) as well as well-marbled beef, some luncheon meats, and bacon.

We've already discussed the fact that healthy eating means sticking to a low-fat, low-salt diet. It *is* better for your heart and for your weight goal to limit fat and salt. But you can't cut out fat completely, any more than you can cut out sugar completely—and if you're eating in an unrestrained manner, there's no reason why you can't fit these foods into your schedule. Because you're monitoring your food intake *weekly* instead of daily, you can always balance your allotment of fat.

Take, for example, a typical fast-food sandwich:

McDonald's Big Mac: 570 calories

35 grams of fat

979 mg. sodium

103 mg. cholesterol

Since fat has 9 calories per gram, we multiply 35 grams by 9 to find out that there are 315 calories of fat in this burger. If you're trying to average around 1,500 calories a day, with 30 percent of those calories coming from fat, you can certainly spare the 315 calories of fat one day—as long as you continue to balance this meal with good low-fat complex carbohydrate meals on most of the other days of your week. The 103 mg. of cholesterol is well within your daily range as well.

But there's a slight hitch. You'd better think twice before adding extras to this burger. Look at the counts:

Serving of fries: 220 calories

12 grams of fat

109 mg. sodium

9 mg. cholesterol

Chocolate shake: 383 calories

9 grams of fat

300 mg. sodium

419 mg. cholesterol

Total meal:	1,173 calories
	(504 of these calories from fat, which is a full day's worth.)
	1,388 mg. sodium
	531 mg. cholesterol

This doesn't mean you can never have an entire fast-food meal, but it does mean you'll have to be careful with the rest of your intake for the next few days so as not to exceed your limits. If you think first and order intelligently, you can satisfy your desire for fast food without going overboard.

You may now begin to add fats and fast food to your weekly intake. You should, of course, be careful about alternating days when you include sweets and days when you include fats.

Tips on Fast Food

1. Make substitutions in your fast-food meal. If you're having a cheese and fat meal such as pizza, stay away from adding red meat (e.g., pepperoni or sausage). If you're having fried food and meat (the burger), cut down on the dairy and cheese. A quarter-pounder without cheese, a regular order of fries, and a diet cola are about 526 calories and 20 grams of fat *less* than the Big Mac, fries, and shake meal.
2. If you think the burger alone won't satiate you, remember that fast-food restaurants offer salads, which will give a filling, lower-calorie component to your meal.
3. Save your fast-food meal for a liberal day, when you're having more calories anyway. If Tuesday is a normally busy day when you don't have time to eat much, make that a low-intake day and stay away from fast food, even though it may be convenient. On Saturday, when you'll eat three full meals, you can have fast food for your

largest meal and you'll be ingesting the same calories and fats you would have on any average liberal day.
4. Remember that you don't have to finish every last bit of fast food on the tray. If your hunger is satisfied, stop eating.

Nighttime Eating

Restrained eaters may somehow find that they are able to go all day without food, but when the sun goes down, their hunger level goes up. They're desperate to make up for all the deprivation they've suffered for the past twelve hours. To many people it seems safer to eat at night because morning will come soon—which means another opportunity for dieting, another chance to erase all the bad memories and indulgences of the previous day. Another typical pattern for restrained eaters is to hide their eating from their families, which is easier to do at night when children are in bed and spouses may be reading the paper or watching TV.

Nighttime eating is not a normal and natural response to the biological needs of your body. Rather, it's an abnormal pattern brought on by years of inappropriate restrained eating. It can certainly wreak havoc with weight maintenance and should be carefully monitored.

Although you're now eating sensibly throughout the day, regulating your intake with your hunger and satiety scales —and although exercise has undoubtedly made a difference in the timing of your hunger—you may still find that old habits die hard. You may still feel hungrier after dinner than you were all day.

The solution is simple: Eat fruit first. Fruit is loaded with sugar, which will satisfy your craving for sweets, and it's also filling and high in fiber, so it takes the body considerable time to digest it. The slower the digestion process, the longer you feel full.

*After your piece of fruit, wait the magic fifteen minutes.
If you are still hungry, you may eat a reasonable portion
of whatever you crave.*

Chances are you'll be too full to eat anything else; but if
you really feel you must have that cupcake or piece of chocolate, don't worry. Because you have eaten the fruit, and
because fifteen minutes have elapsed, your brain's satiety
signals will be working; and that will keep your eating under
control.

Why You Love
Certain Foods and How You
Can Get Your Fill

Food isn't appealing only because it tastes good—it's also
irresistible if the texture is wonderful or the smell drives you
wild. On the negative side, some people can't even think
about eating an oyster, not because of the way it tastes but
because of the way it feels in the mouth. Others can't get a
glass of buttermilk near their lips because the smell is over-
powering. The same is true with foods that you're crazy about.
The taste itself may be an insignificant part of the whole
experience of seeing the food, smelling it, feeling it on your
lips and tongue.

You probably never stop to think about why you'd walk a
mile for an ice-cream cone or a bag of potato chips; but if
you do a little analysis of your own likes and dislikes, you
may be able to find palatable foods that you can substitute
for foods like those after you've finished your reasonable
portion of them. Let's examine a few examples:

1. *Ice Cream*: It's cool, it's creamy, it's sweet, it melts in
   your mouth. Do you think, perhaps, that a slice of *hon-
   eydew melon* might resemble it?
2. *Pumpkin Pie*: It's rich and filling and smells wonderful

when it's baking. An *acorn squash* baked with orange juice and spiced with cinnamon might not be dessert, but it does have a similar texture and odor.

3. *Potato Chips*: The crispy crunch and salty flavor are out of this world. *A celery stick with garlic powder* might be a replacement. Or consider *air-popped popcorn sprinkled with a favorite spice.*

You can think up dozens of these—some will work for you better than others. They won't be the real thing, but there's no reason why you can't have both of such a pair of foods. They'd balance each other nicely, as a matter of fact.

Think and Feel Your Hunger, Don't Plan It

Don't get obsessive about when to eat fast food, sweets, or snacks. If you use the principles you've learned—hunger and satiety, pacing, portion control, and weekly caloric maintenance—you'll never go overboard. (See Steps III, IV, and V if you need a review.)

By now, your sensible eating and exercise, and your new adaptive habits, should have convinced you that you are and will always be an unrestrained eater. I'm sure you can now handle sweets, snacks, fats, and fast food—and enjoy them, too. By giving up the notion that there will always be certain things you aren't allowed to eat, you've done yourself an enormous favor. You've completely liberalized your eating and proven beyond the shadow of a doubt that when food is forbidden, it always tastes sweeter—and only causes you to gain weight.

DIGESTIBLES

1. The only thing that "trigger" foods unleash is the psychological feeling of restraint. If you become an unrestrained eater, you can eat a little of everything.

2. Five bites of any desired food, from ice cream to fast food, will usually satisfy your mouth hunger. If you're still hungry, try eating fruit.

3. Sugar by itself is not bad; only when it's combined with fat does it become calorically dense. So when you crave sweets, have a hard candy instead of a chocolate bar.

4. Rinse your mouth after eating sweets to prevent cavities.

5. Work your fast foods into your liberal-day schedule to keep fats, sodium, and calories within weekly allotments.

Step VIII.
The Exercise Challenge—
Working Toward Goals

Over the past two months, you've probably begun to notice that exercise has changed your body. You may not be exactly sure how, but you're aware that your clothes fit differently and that the muscles under your skin have more definition and strength. Your clothes may not be looser, unless you're still actively engaged in losing weight, but they seem to lie more gracefully on you.

Now that you see where exercise has brought you, you may want more. You may think that greater muscle definition will add immeasurably to your self-image, or that strength and flexibility will add to your athletic potential. This is certainly true. As long as you keep your goals in perspective and realize that you cannot alter your genetic inheritance, you may now begin to open up some new doors to your physical prowess and progress.

The Reward of More Exercise

The truth is that most post-fasters are not really going to be very interested in competing in the Iron Man Triathalon or even in running a marathon. The intense physical labor (and pain) involved is beyond the desire and ability of the average daily athlete. It's probable, however, that some of you are now hooked on exercise and want to go further. You believe that if you feel this good from running two miles a day, you might feel twice as good if you placed in a 10K race. And if you just beat your younger business partner in racquetball for the first time, you might see yourself entering a racquetball tournament in the not-too-distant future.

If you're up to it, I say, go for it! Just the idea of training for that race, or plunging in at that swim meet, or taking a ribbon in the finals of your league's volleyball tournament, may get you to another point in your development, both physically and psychologically.

In training for a competition, there are a few basic rules to follow. Let's consider running a race, the most common example:

1. Step up your regular workouts gradually. If you generally run two miles a day, and you're going to race six (about ten kilometers), you should add half a mile every four or five days. At some point before the race, you might want to complete the whole course, though it's not absolutely necessary. You can finish a 10k race if you've

averaged two and a half miles a day, six days a week, for the last six to eight weeks prior to the race.

2. Try jogging while carrying light hand-weights, to increase the difficulty of the run.
3. Run different courses in training, taking some up- and downhill work as well as flats.
4. Do some interval training. Long, slow running will give you endurance, and a few sprints will teach you to continue to run while in pain.
5. During the race, pace yourself—hold yourself back from where you think you should be in the pack. Never sprint at the beginning; you want to save that for the last quarter of a mile.

If you're into swimming or long-distance biking, you'll also have to increase your pace gradually. If you're a racquet-sport enthusiast, the club or gym you belong to will probably offer clinics or opportunities for advanced training. If you're in the martial arts, your goals are defined for you—your teacher or sensei will determine when you're ready to be tested and to go on to the next level.

Human beings seem to respond better to challenge when there's a carrot at the end of that stick. If you do decide to expand your exercise horizons, be sure you pamper yourself with an extra-special reward. For example:

Exercise challenge: Finishing a 10k race
Reward: Two nights at a country inn

Exercise challenge: A trophy in racquetball
Reward: New speakers or CD player for your stereo system

Exercise challenge: Getting through Jane Fonda's advanced workout
Reward: A new, revealing outfit

An additional reward, and something that's very good for you as well, is to get pampered every once in a while with a steambath, and/or a sauna and a professional massage and rubdown. Competing feels wonderful when you've never done it before; and getting the kinks out afterward can feel even better.

Body Shaping

It may be depressing to see your weight going down on the scale and feel your capacity for exercise increase, but to have to acknowledge that your upper arms are still flabby and the cellulite bumps on your thighs are as pronounced as ever. Why do you lose fat only where it doesn't count? How do you get a perfectly proportioned body?

In most cases, the answer is that you don't. Madison Avenue may try to convince you that you can achieve one, but its claims for certain wonder creams and tonics are as fallacious as the next miracle diet. Spot reduction—by rubbing, bumping, lifting, or manipulating flesh—just doesn't work. Even selectively and vigorously exercising a certain body part won't result in special fat loss in that area. It will tone the muscle underneath, but it won't disperse the fat in any different pattern.

The reason for this unfortunate human phenomenon is that the body can't be made to selectively lose fat from any particular area just because you pay more attention to it. When the body burns calories, it's blind. It burns them all over—not in the place you'd like it to.

There are two types of cell membranes in body fat—those rich in *alpha receptors* and those rich in *beta receptors*. The betas are far more resistant to surrendering their fat stores because they serve as one of the body's survival mechanisms, protecting fuel for times of famine. On a woman, the betas are usually located in the hips, buttocks, and thighs. (Mother Nature apparently planned it this way so that a woman could still conceive and nurture infants, even if half-starved herself.) On a man, the betas are mostly located in the abdomen.

These stubborn fat deposits are genetically determined. A

program of overall weight reduction and a general exercise plan will naturally reduce some of the beta-receptors, but they'll never go away completely.

Now let's look at cellulite, the bane of many women's existence. Contrary to popular opinion, cellulite is not a special kind of fat. It's just normal body fat (frequently located in an area rich in beta-receptor fat) with a genetically determined pattern of connective tissue overlay that causes the characteristic orange-peel look.

There are various salons that treat cellulite with chemical preparations, electrical and manual stimulation, and diet, but the truth is that there isn't very much that can be done. If you now happen to be a skinny woman on top with well-defined clavicles and a wasp waist, but you still have saddlebags down below, it's something you're just going to have to learn to live with—to a certain extent.

The picture isn't completely bleak. You can tone and shape your body with *anaerobic exercise*, and in many instances this can make an enormous difference. This other form of exercise—moving against resistance—is one way of using the fitness level you already have to make your body more responsive in other areas.

Anaerobic Workouts

Running, swimming, and other aerobic exercises depend on fixed resistance—that is, as much as you work out, you're always contracting your muscles against the same amount of resistance. But in order to strengthen your muscles and make them more flexible, you have to use *dynamic resistance*, moving a resistant mass with the muscle you're training.

The mass can be your own body (as in push-ups and pull-ups); the resistance can be your own muscles pushing against each other (as in isometrics); but the most common form of anaerobics is weight training, either with free weights or Nautilus-type equipment. The idea is that the more you stress your muscles by overloading them with resistance, the stronger they get.

The increase that occurs in a muscle's size when it's stressed is known as hypertrophy. If you make the muscle under the skin larger, it changes the shape of that area of the body. Look at Mr. Universe if you want to see the questionably impressive results of hypertrophying muscles to an extreme degree. But you don't need to go that far. When used in combination with your regular aerobic fitness program, under the close supervision of a trained instructor, a workout on a Nautilus or its equivalent can start to define the areas of your body that you want to emphasize, and downplay those that you feel are too large or out of shape.

On a Nautilus, which is multistation equipment, you have a number of machines designed to exercise specific muscles. These various stations help to give the body an overall toning and to build strength, endurance, and flexibility—all vital not just for your body's esthetics, but certainly also for facilitating any and all aerobic exercise you're involved in.

Free-weight lifting, which should be attempted only at a gym with a qualified instructor, is another way of getting an anaerobic workout. It works on three principles: overload, progression, and balance.

When you work your muscles at near-maximum strength, or *overload* them, the muscles respond according to the demand placed on them. It's more beneficial, anaerobically speaking, to do five to ten reps (or repetitions) at your maximum effort than fifteen to twenty reps at only 50 percent of your capacity. Remember, this is the absolute opposite of pacing yourself in aerobic exercise—don't ever confuse the two.

Each time you do an anaerobic workout, you must think about *progression*. You add to the weight you're lifting as you gain strength. If you started at ten reps with one hundred pounds, you might next tackle ten reps with one hundred and ten pounds.

Finally, in order to prevent injury, your goal is to develop your extensor and flexor muscles proportionally to keep *balance* around a joint. When you work all your body parts an equal amount, you'll have total balance.

Although anaerobic exercise is a nice extra because you can really see the results of your labor, it can never replace aerobic exercise for weight control and total body fitness. There are also a few contraindications you should be aware of.

1. *Lower-back problems.* If you've had a lower-back injury or have been prone to weakness in this area, weight lifting is not for you. Even with close supervision, it's easy to attempt a lift at the wrong angle or with poor lifting form, or to take on just too much weight for your capacity and throw your whole body out of alignment.
2. *Knee problems.* Most lifters wear knee pads, which is some protection, but you can easily contract tendonitis or other knee injuries despite your precautions.
3. *Shoulder and upper-arm pain.* Trying to progress too fast can worsen these pains.

A brief warning about steroids: When you're around a gym that specializes in weight training, you're sure to run into a few lifters who have taken anabolic steroids and who counsel you to try them. These are artificial male sex hormones that speed up muscle growth and bulk. They can have disastrous side-effects, from lower sperm counts in men to male-patterned baldness in women. They tend to raise cholesterol levels, and they can cause severe psychological problems.

I must repeat once more that exercise can only tone and strengthen muscles. It does nothing for the connective tissue or the fat below it. This means that only a program of continued weight loss or maintenance—depending on your goals—and daily aerobic exercise is going to make any difference in the general conditioning of your body. The *contour* of your body is something else again. The long, lean line of the fashion model or the rock star may simply not be within your reach. However there *is* a final alternative to body shaping, as discussed in the following paragraphs—but it's not for everyone.

Surgery—The Final Option

Many people who've lost a significant amount of weight are saddened and sometimes infuriated to discover that their skin doesn't spring back or lie flat and tight when they've slimmed down. Years of stretching the skin over layers of fat has reduced its elasticity. The only possible way to deal with this problem is surgery.

In this operation, a skilled plastic surgeon removes the excess skin and stretches the existing tissue back into shape. The decision to make this drastic alteration in your physical appearance is a very personal one and should not be taken lightly. It's very expensive and the results are not always guaranteed. Medical insurance may not cover this procedure.

If you are really committed to doing this, you should discuss it with your personal physician first and get his referral to a qualified plastic surgeon. This is far preferable to simply picking your own plastic surgeon by word of mouth or through an advertisement. The Madison Avenue hard-sell has, unfortunately, entered the world of plastic surgery, and it's easy to be lured into a hasty decision by rash promises and miracle claims.

When you've found a doctor you trust, ask to see his "before and after" pictures for similar surgery. Most important, you should ask for a realistic assessment of your particular problem and a truthful prediction of what the outcome of such surgery on your particular problem might be.

There's another procedure that many post-fasters express interest in, and this is liposuction, in which fat is actually sucked out of the body. The only areas that should be treated this way are those small, beta-rich, selective areas of bulging fat—like the saddlebag bulges on the outer thighs—that are completely resistant to diet and exercise.

Again, you must consider the various dangers of such surgery, and balance them against the benefits. There are a variety of risks whenever you disrupt the blood and nerve supply to the skin, and, of course, there's a real risk every time you submit to general anesthesia.

You should keep in mind that liposuction is *not* a method of weight reduction, but is a serious surgical step that should be taken only after much thought and with responsible professional consultation.

Reassessing Your
Long-Term Weight Goals

Many weeks ago, you consulted the chart on pages 30–31 and decided what weight goal was comfortable for you. You continued your sensible eating and daily exercise with the thought that this goal might be just a temporary stopping place. Maybe you really wanted to get into a pair of size 10 jeans, and assumed that by the ninth week of your maintenance program you'd be able to burn all your old "fat" clothes. Maybe you initially imagined yourself so extraordinarily in shape that you would have reset your setpoint about ten pounds lower than your original ideal weight goal.

Maybe that's happened—but maybe it hasn't. This is an excellent time to look at where you are and where you're going. Ask yourself the following questions:

1. Have you gained weight since you stopped fasting and started eating and exercising?
2. If so, has it come back rapidly?
3. Have you stayed the same? Does this same weight feel different because of your new body awareness?
4. Have you lost weight? If so, has it come off quickly or slowly? Have you reached a plateau and found you can't lose any more?

The answers to these questions indicate your body's true nature, a genetic message that you simply can't ignore. There are, as you know, biological factors that are out of your control and that have a strong influence on your total body fat. You can certainly play with these factors—you can and probably have reset your setpoint downward since you've been on this program.

But your body has its own natural limitations. Perhaps you've found that in order to maintain the goal weight you set eight weeks ago, you must contend with the following problems.

- You had to eat less than your allotted 1,100 or 1,400 daily calories during that phase of the program.
- You are having real fears about forbidden foods.
- You are rigorously exercising and still cannot eat what you want.

If so, you may have to set yourself a higher target weight.

It won't be much higher than the range you originally set—perhaps ten pounds or so—but that can make a huge difference in how much you can eat and how comfortable you feel with your hunger and satiety. By continuing your exercise and liberalizing your diet, you'll find out just where your natural plateau is. That's the weight at which your body is going to feel best.

I hope this news won't depress you—and in the final chapter, we're going to talk about accepting and even liking your stable weight. The point is that to be a person who no longer worries about weight and who lives by the practice of sensible eating and exercising, you may have to be a person who's basically not skinny. Remember that "normal" has nothing to do with a number on the scale—it has a lot more to do with a way of life and a sound philosophy of good health that's right for you.

If, on the other hand, you have been losing more weight since you stopped fasting, you should know that you'll reach a plateau eventually. Wait to buy your new wardrobe until you've leveled off and stayed approximately the same weight for at least two months.

If you've taken on a really difficult exercise schedule, working toward a goal such as a marathon or a long-distance swimming or bike race, you may find over the course of your training that even though you're burning more calories, you're not losing more weight. The reason for this is that you're gaining muscle mass, and muscle weighs more than fat. Rest assured that your weight will stabilize and your shape will improve because of your increased muscle tone.

I told you there were no magical solutions to weight maintenance, and the fact that you can't change your body beyond a certain point can be a tough one to accept. There just aren't that many perfect bodies in the world. There are, however, ways of reaching complete contentment with the body you've got and complete satisfaction with the results of your efforts to keep it in good shape.

The ultimate challenge is to like yourself and the world around you. And the last step of the *After the Fast* program is going to help you do just that.

DIGESTIBLES

1. Working toward a difficult exercise challenge such as a race or tournament can be an exciting adjunct to your regular eating and exercise program.

2. Body shaping is possible—within your own genetically determined limitations—with the addition of anaerobic exercise to your aerobic exercise schedule.

3. Nautilus and free-weight programs must be closely supervised to prevent injury.

4. Plastic surgery should be considered only as a last resort, for those who are very unhappy with draping skin or resistant fat bulges.

5. You may need to reassess your weight goals. It's perfectly all right to find that your body is more comfortable with a few more pounds than you had originally planned to weigh.

Step IX.
Keys to New Self-Esteem

Why are we all obsessed with being thin? Why is physical appearance so crucial in our evaluation of ourselves and the way we deal with the world? Why can't we wake up one morning and truly believe that it's more important to be accepted for who we are than for how we look?

The answer is not an easy one, because much as we all pay lip service to being above petty vanity, to being concerned with higher or better things than mere appearance, our culture has shaped and molded us in a certain direction. We live in an era in which tyranny reigns in the name of "thin and beautiful."

And those who suffer from weight problems are among its worst victims. Henry VIII may have been the greatest example of power and sexuality in the Renaissance, but in 1990 America he would be labeled "fat," with all the unsavory connotations that go along with that word. It doesn't matter that scientists have proven that the human body's proclivity to put on weight has a strong biological determinant; despite that, an obese figure today connotes to many of us an image of slovenliness, low self-esteem, gluttony, and lack of personal control. If Henry were currently running for office, his media managers would undoubtedly suggest a fast and a maintenance program for him.

The tyranny of the thin goes beyond tormenting only those who tip the scales at an unfashionably high weight. As a postfaster, you too are persecuted. You still bear the psychological scars of once having been overweight. As we proved in Step V and are about to demonstrate once again, these scars don't melt away with your unwanted pounds. Even though you may not have a weight problem any longer, you probably still think as though you do, and you may still believe that society holds you in lesser esteem because of your former physical condition.

You've been working hard on developing counter-beliefs about dieting and weight loss. In Step IX, we're going to start breaking down your old maladaptive habits and beliefs about yourself and the world around you. These are the toughest of all false beliefs to change, but you're ready for that challenge now because you've already accomplished so much in your maintenance program.

You know by now that your psychological reality is based on the way you think about yourself. In order for your eating and exercising to make a real difference in your life, you have

to alter your old psychological reality, stripping it of its irrational and negative components. This is the *only* way you're
going to maintain the weight you have now for the rest of
your life and acknowledge that it's the right weight for you.

Changes in Attitude Make
Changes in Behavior Possible

When you have a new perspective on an old problem, it gives
you a way to do something about that problem. Without a
fresh outlook, you can never modify your behavior because
your attitudes and beliefs are simply too powerful—they can
overwhelm every effort you make to change. If you still sub-
scribe to irrational beliefs about your body and its impact
on every other aspect of your life, those old unhappy, anxious
feelings you used to have will slowly and insidiously creep
back in, undermining your new resolve *not* to use food as a
solution or a palliative.

In this section we describe six major irrational beliefs that
may stand in the way of your lifetime of good health. Begin
to tackle them now, realizing that they're not going to dis-
appear overnight. But although you can't expect immediate
gratification, I promise that you *will* see the results you
want—a good weight you can live with and no further ob-
sessions about dieting.

Remember the valuable techniques we used in Step VI to
help modify and alter your old attitudes? These are your
guideposts for the final work of your maintenance program:

1. rational, adaptive *counter-beliefs*
2. therapeutic *exercises* for each irrational belief
3. *reminder cards* in purse, pocket, and on the refrigerator

And now, we are going to add a fourth, relaxation technique, to help you more comfortably accept new beliefs and
attitudes into your life.

Correcting False Beliefs
About the World Around Us

Let's address three major irrational beliefs you are likely to hold about the world, and three about yourself. Somewhere, they all overlap, which is what's made them so difficult and confusing to you for so long. Right now, we're going to unravel them and deal with each belief in a concrete, functional manner.

Irrational Belief I. *The world ought to be fair.* If you've had a weight problem, this belief reasserts itself every time you see a thin person sit down and eat an enormous meal (including dessert) without thinking twice about it. You feel cheated, overlooked, and dealt a terrible hand by fate. *Why can't I eat all I want without gaining weight?* you probably ask. Why can't the world accept me just as I am? Why do I have to live with the stigma of being fat? It's so unfair! Why can't the world be fair?

If you think this way, you're naturally going to be depressed about your lot in life. Those feelings of depression and doubt, the nagging question, "Is it all worth it?" can wipe out the best intentions to stick with a sensible exercise and eating program.

Exercise

Count your gratitudes.

1. Accept reality. You just have to acknowledge that life isn't fair. Rather, it's a complex combination of forces and powers, some of which are completely out of our hands but many of which we can control.
2. Learn to use the control you do have to examine your life objectively, and congratulate yourself for your attributes.
3. *Use your gratitudes.* Each of us has a few special talents, attributes, and skills that no one else can claim. Maybe your weight always has been a problem, but on the other

hand, maybe no one else in the world has your facility for languages, or your fabulous red-gold hair, or your ability to run a corporation. For another source of gratitudes think of the many times you've heard about a tragic accident and been enormously grateful that you were you, safe and sound. I want you to fill in the blanks in the following statements to determine where your particular gratitudes lie:

I.   I don't have a perfect body, but something I do have

    is _____.

II. I can't eat all I want and stay skinny, but something

    I *can* do is _____.

III. I may not lead a glamorous, movie-star life, but something terrific I do on a regular basis is

    _____.

IV. All heads might not turn when I walk into a room, but they would be impressed if they knew that I

    _____.

V.   I may not be "number one" in all things but I *feel* like number one when it comes to

    _____.

Interesting, isn't it? You really do have a few areas that belong exclusively to you, that give you pleasure and pride in yourself. The battle of the bulge, as we proved in Step VI, doesn't have to be fought day and night, on every front, because it really isn't the centerpiece of your self-esteem.

New Belief

No, all right, the world isn't fair, but I have much to be grateful for and things could be a lot worse.

Irrational Belief 2. *I am the center of attention.* Every summer, as you venture onto the beach wearing your bathing suit for the first time that season, do you know in your heart that everyone on the beach—every single person—came out that day *just* to see *you*? Not one of them had any interest in swimming or sunbathing—it was all just a ruse so they could scrutinize and criticize *your* body in *your* swimsuit.

Are you smiling because you think it's ridiculous? Or are you laughing because it hurts too much to cry? We all believe it! We really do! As ludicrous as it might seem, most of us are fixed on the belief that all eyes are focused on us, and that our appearance is really of primary importance to other people. One of the most torturous results of having once been overweight is the sense that "the whole world is watching"—and judging.

There's nothing funny about the consequence of this belief, which keeps so many formerly overweight people away from the pool and the beach, from exercise classes where dress-code calls for a leotard, even from parties and reunions where revealing or tight-fitting clothing isn't an issue.

Objectively, you must know that people are much too busy with their own lives to be deeply invested in the way you look. This is certainly true of strangers and acquaintances, and even friends and neighbors. (We deal with your immediate family later, in the discussion of another belief.)

The following exercise—which does involve a bit of risk-taking—will prove to you that you are not the center of attention.

Exercise

1. You're going to purposely put yourself into a situation that makes you uncomfortable—be it the beach, the pool, the exercise class, the class reunion, or the office party.
2. Select a situation where there will be a lot of people present, not an intimate gathering. If you can, take a friend with you.
3. When at the event, consciously make an effort to stand outside yourself and your embarrassed feelings. Pretend that you are a journalist taking notes on the scene. As a detached, *objective* observer, you are going to watch

people watching you and see just how much attention
they really pay you. (If you've come with a friend, you
can start your experiment by watching people watching
him or her—which will initially take the burden of self-
consciousness out of the exercise.)
4. In your mind, make a triple-column list. On the left, put
a check every time a person completely ignores you,
either because he's wrapped up in conversation or because he's simply not interested. In the middle, put a
check every time a person gives you a passing glance.
On the right, check when you get a real stare.

Yes, you'll have a few checks in the right-hand column—
you do live in a weight-obsessed society, and there are those
insecure types who need to feel they are superior to anyone
and everyone. They generally stare at others in order to make
comparisons with their own looks. But chances are your
checks will be heaviest on the left and in the middle. If you
get looks, they'll probably be brief because the looker will
return quickly to more pressing matters.

New Belief
The truth is that everyone is his or her own center of attention
and doesn't have time to pay that much attention to your
appearance. Most people don't care how you look.

Reminder Card
Write yourself the following corrective sentence and carry it
with you. Post it on your refrigerator so you can practice it
at home: *"If they don't like my body, that's their problem,
not mine!"*

Irrational Belief 3. *I must be accepted and admired by everyone.* This belief is a corollary to the one we just dispensed
with. It runs like this: *"If I am the center of attention, then I
must be accepted and admired by those paying attention to
me."*

It's easy to see how we've all been gulled by this one. It's reinforced every day, in so many ways, in the world around us. After all, our culture worships heroes, which means we all grow up wanting to *be* heroes. Whether the adulation goes to movie stars or athletes, it's the same—they're larger-than-life figures (made even larger by the media) who all of us little guys can admire and envy. How fascinated we are when our heroes fall from grace—we gobble up news about their scandalous doings which prove that even they are fallible.

For this reason, we all aspire to gain our own corner of "celebrity" by being accepted and admired by others. And physical attractiveness is one quick route to admiration—as well as the jealousy and envy we secretly relish. Unfortunately, overweight people are rarely, if ever, admired for being physically appealing. But then, many thin people miss that goal, too. Being beautiful doesn't always come with being thin.

One consequence of craving love and admiration is the need to please everyone. If you're a "people-pleaser," you may bend over backwards to do things for others in the vain hope that they'll like you. But you can't please all the people all the time. There's only one individual who must be pleased, and that's yourself.

The problem for many formerly overweight people is that in order to please themselves, to gain self-acceptance and self-admiration, they have to learn to like something they've always hated—their bodies. If you've always thought of your body as your major handicap, if even now—after losing a substantial amount of weight—you still talk about your "disgusting thighs" and "gross gut," you need a fresh perspective on the way you look *now*. It's practically impossible to get to like your body when you can't see it objectively.

Exercise

You're going to work on *body-image distortion*. This is a very prevalent problem in which overweight and reduced-weight people often see themselves as fatter than they really are. This is an illusion that takes place in front of a mirror—the same mirror that used to reflect back a fat person—and it can cause acute despair and self-reproach, as well as another round of desperate dieting.

1. Ask your spouse or a good friend to take a set of photographs. You should pose for front, side, and rear shots, first wearing a nice outfit, then a bathing suit. Be sure you've combed your hair and, if you're a woman, put on a little make-up. If you have access to a video camera, by all means get yourself filmed as well, but you also need the still photos.

2. Study the pictures, paying special attention to the good points revealed by the camera. Then examine the areas you feel are flawed, but try to be objective about them, too. Is your rear really "as big as a house" or not so bad? Does your stomach still stick out, or is it now much flatter than it used to be?

3. Get out some pictures from before your fast to make a comparison. Before-and-after photography can reveal astonishing differences. You will probably begin to admire and accept the new you much more readily when you see how far you've come.

4. Compare your photos to those in newspapers and magazines (not fashion magazines). Have you possibly been too harsh in front of your mirror?

5. Finally, stand in front of the mirror with a before and after photo on either side of you. Do you have a less distorted image of your body now? Do you like it a little better? Liking yourself is a wonderful feeling—one you could certainly get used to.

Reminder Card

Write yourself the following statement and carry it with you: *"I must work on self-acceptance and admiration—good things will follow from the belief that I have a lot of strong points."* Below this, write yourself a list of all the good things you've done and are doing for your appearance and health. On the flip side of the card, make a list of the many other good things in your life, as well as your personal and professional achievements.

New Belief
Universal acceptance and admiration is an illusion created by the media. Personal acceptance is what I ought to strive for.

Beliefs About Yourself and Your Self-Worth

Irrational Belief 1. *I am unattractive and undesirable.* One of the heaviest pieces of emotional baggage the overweight or reduced-weight person carries is an enduring sense of being unattractive and sexually undesirable. This isn't a totally irrational belief, because in most human societies, if your appearance doesn't coincide with the current ideals, you may not be considered *visually* desirable by many.

This isn't to say that intimacy and sexuality can't be important parts of your life; rather, it's a realistic acknowledgment of all the negative reinforcement you've probably gotten in the area of casual sexual attractiveness—which usually isn't the area that counts in the long run, by the way.

The post-faster, who's gone from one body to another, may have particular problems stemming from a changing body image and all that it implies. After all, being fat was one way to insulate and protect yourself from having to deal with sexual pressure. If no one ever approached you, you might have felt invulnerable, an island unto yourself.

But now, as you emerge from the cocoon in which you had previously isolated yourself, you may find that the new attention you're getting isn't entirely welcome. It can feel very threatening to realize that your spouse or lover or casual acquaintance finds your thinner, more muscular body more desirable. The attention you're getting and the intense feelings that come along with intimacy can make you feel vulnerable, exposed, and ill-equipped to deal with the new nature of your relationships.

These problems are far too complex and challenging to be solved in this book. But you can use your understanding about the power of beliefs and attitudes to get started in the right direction, and begin to question your long-standing feelings about being unattractive and undesirable.

Exercise 1
Do the absolute best with what you've got.

Give some thought to the externals—grooming and clothing. Now that you've made such strides with eating and exercise, you deserve a few treats.

1. If you've settled into your setpoint, buy yourself a few new outfits.
2. Get a new hairstyle, a manicure, a make-up consultation, a day of beauty treatments at the best spa in town. Get pampered like this often—it will go a long way toward diminishing any lingering feelings of unattractiveness.

Exercise 2
Learn to relax.

It may make you feel anxious just to consider the possibility of sex after the fast. If you're married, and your spouse is suddenly more turned on by the new you, you may feel confused about how a renewed sexual connection will affect the other facets of your marriage. If you're single and find yourself suddenly being pursued, you may feel awkward and uncomfortable in social situations. None of the old rules apply any more—so which rules are you supposed to play by?

By practicing relaxation techniques *before* an anticipated difficult experience, you'll increase your self-confidence and significantly improve your chances of a good outcome to the event. After all, we fear the unknown—but we can handle the expected.

1. Find a quiet, comfortable place and sit or lie down, closing your eyes. Focus on taking slow, deep breaths.

Inhale through your nose; exhale through your mouth.

2. Consciously tense and then relax each part of your body, beginning with your toes and working slowly up toward your head. Hold the tension for a count of three, then release for another three, and so on.

3. While in this relaxed state, visualize and vividly imagine the frightening or stressful intimate situation. As you do this, begin to introduce positive outcomes to replace the negative ones you anticipate. For example:

   • The "attractive" man or woman does not reject your attempt at casual conversation; instead, he or she welcomes and continues it.

   • Your lovemaking with your spouse or lover is free and spontaneous, not anxious and uptight as you had feared.

4. Use these fantasies again during the actual situation— and understand that although they won't work magic and may not work every time, they *will* help you to reshape the outcome of your intimate experiences.

New Belief

"I'm not unattractive and undesirable. I'm a fox! I'm a hunk!"

Irrational Belief 2: *I am responsible for other people's feelings.* To a certain extent, it's fine and good to feel that you want to make the important others in your life happy. You do have a stake in your relationships with your spouse, children, parents, and friends, and part of holding up your end is doing things that will nourish those relationships and cause them to grow.

But suppose you are continually barraged with criticism from the ones you're trying to please. Suppose that no matter how hard you try, you can't change enough to please them. Are you responsible for the way they feel? If your spouse wasn't happy about your body before your fast, and you stuck to your guns and lost weight and exercised and he *still* isn't happy about your body, is that your fault?

No, it most certainly isn't. The overweight person in our

society generally suffers from guilt, shame, and shattered personal self-esteem. It's an additional burden, then, to feel responsible for disappointing family and friends, for letting them down by not being sufficiently thin and sexy—if those are the attributes they find so important.

If you're a post-faster, this situation can be particularly difficult. It must be extremely frustrating to feel—after you've lost a considerable amount of weight—that your family is *still* disappointed in you. Thankfully, because of your own work on changing your attitudes and increasing your self-esteem, you're getting over your feelings of unattractiveness. But how are you going to deal with the feelings of those around you, when their implied criticism or outright sarcasm threatens to undermine your new belief that pleasing yourself is the only thing that counts?

Exercise

You're going to bring the question of weight and attractiveness out of the closet and attack the problem head-on with honesty. Lovers and spouses may talk about many things together, but they tend to avoid discussions of whether or not they find each other physically appealing. Instead, they'll give off signals—hopefully positive ones that encourage intimacy, but very often negative ones that may turn their partners off and create distance between them.

If you're a weight-reduced woman getting the message from your spouse that you've done a wonderful job and are very much to be admired, you'll probably have no problem staying with your maintenance plan. But if your spouse ignores your success or even jokes about how far your are from your goal, and if you persist in accepting the guilt for having a less-than-perfect body, you're buying into the maladaptive belief that you're responsible for his feelings.

I want to urge you *not* to accept this guilt, because the negative feelings it will bring on can induce you to resort to old habits—dieting and then gorging yourself, and ceasing to exercise, because you figure that, after all, if you can't get a kind word from your spouse it's not worth trying so hard to be different.

Instead of accepting this guilt, you must confront the problem and sit down for an honest discussion with your spouse.

1. Prepare yourself with the relaxation exercise you just learned. If you anticipate ridicule or criticism, substitute visual and auditory imagery of a successful and meaningful conversation.

2. Make an appointment with your spouse for this serious talk. Make sure you will have plenty of time and no distractions.

3. Write yourself a list of issues you want to bring up— even write out statements you intend to make so that you won't forget them in the heat of the moment. For example:

   • "I sense you're still disappointed with my body despite all the weight I've lost.

   • "I really *resent* the fact that you don't appreciate me or my accomplishments."

   • "I've learned to feel good about myself, and that's the most important thing for me."

   • "If you're still going to be unhappy and disappointed, I can't be held responsible for your feelings."

4. Don't be timid. When you confront your spouse, you've got to be honest, no matter how you think it may hurt.

5. If you really fear this encounter, write a detailed note and present it to your significant other, asking for a meeting after he or she has read it and had time to consider it.

If you aren't getting through and the encounters seem to be doing nothing but causing friction between you, I advise you to seek counseling. Professionals are trained to help people open up to each other and learn to communicate. They can also provide a more distanced eye that can see both sides of an issue.

This is not an easy exercise, but it's essential. Touchy subjects like personal appearance and self-esteem can't be avoided or ignored in an honest relationship. And getting through these painful feelings with a loved one may help you pass the final hurdle to being completely comfortable with the improvements you've made so far, and intend to keep making, in your life style.

Irrational Belief 3: *It's too hard to change.* The best resolve to stick with a maintenance program of good health may occasionally be undermined. An illness that keeps you away from exercising, a holiday season that creates an overwhelming urge to eat everything in sight, even a series of unrelated stressful incidents—such things can lead to a sense of futility about all the challenges that lie ahead, and cause you to revert to familiar old patterns of behavior.

In many ways, you are working to recover from a lifetime of bad habits and attitudes just as an alcoholic or drug-addicted individual must do. In my practice as a specialist in addictive behavior, I work with many struggling people who feel overwhelmed by the burden of having to change.

There is nothing easy about recovery, but there are two simple maxims, frequently heard at AA meetings, that I want you to inscribe in your personal book of life. The first is:

Take it easy.

If you can learn to be forgiving of and easy on yourself, you'll be able to come to terms with the fact that no single failure could possibly be sufficient to counteract all the good you've done up to now. No food binge at a wedding, no injury that's kept you from your daily run for a few weeks, can undo the results of your fast and exercise program. Be kinder to yourself and remember that you'll get back on track eventually. Everyone has lapses. Instead of being self-critical for messing up, pat yourself on the back for sticking to your program this long and faithfully. The second maxim is:

One day at a time.

One of the surest ways to feel overwhelmed is to project yourself into the future and start imagining all the roadblocks to behavior change that could possibly lie ahead. Of course it may look hopeless if you think in terms of committing yourself to a totally new way of living for the next ten or twenty years.

But the truth of the matter is that no one can anticipate what problems or pleasures lie ahead—no one knows how hard or easy it's going to be to change and keep changing. You can't anticipate your problems because each day your new behaviors and attitudes are growing stronger and more deeply embedded. This means you're more capable, on a daily basis, of dealing with difficult issues and major crises in your life. What might have seemed like an unreachable goal six months ago—fasting and then staying within range of your post-fast weight—no longer seems like much of a challenge at all. What looks impossible right now—maintaining your new eating and exercising behavior on your annual week away in Mexico—might be easily achievable by the time you board the plane for your vacation.

Focus on *today*, not tomorrow. What about it—did you do your laps today? Did you keep your fats down and your carbs up? Did you think positively about your new self-image? You did? Great!

Tomorrow is another day to take it easy, one day at a time.

A New Structure
to Your Mind and Body

For today and tomorrow and the rest of your life, you have a potential and an opportunity you never had before. You have proved to yourself that you—and only you—have the ability and stamina and will to change, to do things that are

---

FINAL STAGE, PROGRESS REPORT

Eating

1. You realize that there are no forbidden foods—you can now eat anything you want in reasonable portions.

2. You understand now how to satisfy your mouth hunger with five bites, and if you're still hungry, you know you can go on to fruit.

3. You understand that you should be aiming for a high-carb, low-fat diet, but if you stray from the path every once in a while, it won't kill you.

Exercise

1. You realize how great it feels to be in shape and you may feel even better by accelerating your workouts or training for a competition.

2. You understand that body shaping can go only so far. You can tone the muscles beneath the skin, but you can't alter genetically determined connective tissue and fat.

3. You understand that anaerobic exercise may add to

---

good for yourself, to realize and acknowledge that you're a worthwhile and lovable person.

Hunger and satiety, pacing, exercising, eradicating false and maladaptive beliefs, are the building blocks in the new structure that you've begun to create. Now you can see before you the blueprint of a natural, comfortable life in which self-esteem is not based solely on the way you look or the way your overall good appearance and feeling about yourself.

4. You realize that plastic surgery may be a final option for those who've lost a great deal of weight. But you know that it should only be an option for *you* after serious discussion with your personal physician.

Body-Knowledge

1. You know that you need to work on your old beliefs about the world around you and your own self-worth.

2. You realize that when things look most unfair and blackest, you can always count your gratitudes.

3. You understand that your weight and body image are your own business—not dependent on the good feelings of anyone else.

4. You are trying to relax about yourself and can now visualize positive outcomes to previously threatening or stressful situations.

5. You are taking it easy, one day at a time.

others view you—but, rather, a life in which you take care of yourself because it feels good and because you deserve it.

Your body is working for you and it's in sync with a mind filled with more forgiving, more flexible attitudes. The plans are all in place, and you, the architect, are ready. Don't be afraid to try new things, or to build too high. The sky's the limit.

Index

Acceptance (admiration, self-acceptance), psychology of weight maintenance and, 167–70. *See also* Self-esteem

Acorn squash, 144

Activity level, setpoint and metabolism and, 19. *See also* Exercise; Metabolism; Sedentary life style

Addiction: compulsive eating as an, 124–27 (*see also* Compulsive eating); positive, exercise as, 21

Aerobic dance, 95, 104–5, 108–9

Aerobic exercise, 11, 14, 20, 51–52, 53, 95–97, 102–3, 104–5, 111, 128, 149, 150, 151, 156; goal of, 96–97; low-impact, 52, 53; record-keeping and, 107–10

Aikido, 95, 98

Almond Joy, 136

Alpha receptors, 148–49

American Heart Association, 73, 92

Amish, the, 18–19

Anabolic steroids, 151

Anaerobic exercise, 95, 149–52, 156, 173; equipment, 149–50; progression and, 150; workouts, dynamic resistance and, 149–52

Anger, 115, 124, 127

Anxiety, 124, 126, 127, 135, 158

Anorexia, 113

Apples, 35, 65, 82

Asparagus, 76, 82

Attitudes, psychology of weight maintenance and, 114–30; self-defeating,

Attitudes (*Cont.*): correcting, exercises, 114–27, 158–71. *See also* Beliefs; specific kinds, problems

Attractiveness, 165–70

Bagels, 35

Bananas, 35, 36

Basal metabolism, fasting and, 8–9. *See also* Metabolism

Basketball, 22, 95, 98, 102

Beans, 76, 79, 87, 93

Beauty treatments, 166

Beef, 34. *See also* Meat

Behavioral changes, 170–71

Beliefs, psychology of weight maintenance and, 111–30, 173; false (irrational), correcting, exercises, 115–27, 158–71, 173; self-defeating, 114–27, 158–71. *See also* specific kinds, problems

Beta receptors, 148–49

Bicycling, 22, 53, 95, 100, 103–4, 108; clubs, 103–4; equipment, 103; stationary, 53, 95, 100, 103

Big Mac burgers, 20, 140–41

Bingeing (gorging), 6, 12, 15–16, 124, 132; sweets and, 137–38

Bites technique, 138–39, 145, 172

Blood pressure, 4, 5, 32, 53; fiber and, 82. *See also* Hypertension

"Body cultists," 19

Body fat, 7; alpha and beta receptors and, 148–149; attitudes and beliefs on, 11, 28, 113–30, 156, 158–71; body shaping and, 148–49; dieting and, 7 (see also Dieting); exercise and, 17, 148 (see also Exercise); metabolism and, 17–19 (see also Metabolism); setpoint and, 17–19 (see also Setpoint). See also Obesity; Weight; specific problems

Body fitness, food and exercise and, 20–23, 55, 98, 145–52. See also Exercise; specific aspects, problems

Body frame, ideal weight and, 29, 30–31, 32

Body image, 112–30, 158–71, 173; distortions, illusions, 163–64; exercise and, 20–23, 103, 106, 161

Body shaping (body contour): anaerobic workouts and, 149–52; exercise and, 148–49, 156, 172; liposuction and, 152–53; surgery and, 152–53

Boredom, 73, 124, 126, 127

Brain, the, 18, 63–64, 66

Bran: muffins, 14, 79; oat, 82, 83

Bread, 34, 35, 65, 79, 81, 83, 84; whole wheat, 34, 35, 65, 81, 82

Breakfast, 33, 35, 36, 62, 83–84, 86, 89–90

Breathing, exercise and, 44, 51, 52, 54, 96. See also Lungs; Pulmonary function

Broccoli, 82

Bulemics, 113

Burgers, 20, 74, 84, 140–42

Butter, 81, 93

Buttermilk, 74

Calorically dense foods, 80–81, 134, 138; listed, 81. See also Calories; specific foods

Calories, 6–9, 80–81; counting, portion-controlled food amounts instead of, 73, 85–89; energy expenditure and, 16, 18–19; exercise and, 19–24, 44, 94–110; fast foods and, 20, 138, 140–42, 145; fasting and metabolism and, 8–9, 29–30 (see also Fasting; Metabolism); food and exercise exchanges and, 13–24, 86, 94–110; forbidden foods and, 138, 140–42, 145; learning how to eat and, 27–29, 58–71; replacing the liquid-protein diet and, 32–40, 57–71, 72–130; restrained and unrestrained eating and (see Restrained and unrestrained eating); sweets and sugar and, 133–38, 139

Cancer, 82; fiber and, 82

Candy, 81, 132, 139; hard, 136–37, 145

Canned foods, salt in, 74–77

Carbohydrates, 81–82, 172; complex, 39, 73, 81–82, 83–84, 85–87; simple, 134

Cardiac function, 4, 14, 54. See also Heart problems; Heart rate

Cavities (dental caries), 135, 145; preventing, 135, 145

Cellulite, 148, 149

Center of attraction, belief in oneself as the, 160–62

Central sensations, hunger and satiety and, 63–64

Cereals and grains, 14, 33, 34, 35, 36, 37, 78, 79, 81, 82, 84. See also specific foods, kinds

Change, behavioral, 170–71

Cheese, 34, 35, 74, 78, 79, 81, 141. See also specific kinds

Chicken (turkey, poultry), 29, 34, 65, 76, 79, 80, 84, 86, 87; cooking tips, 92–93

Chinese food, 74

Chips, 138, 139. See also Potato chips

Chocolate, 81, 136; milk, 81; shake, 140

Cholesterol, 14, 73, 77; fast foods and, 140–42; fiber and, 82, 83; fish oils and, 80; HDL, 14; restricting, 14, 73, 77, 83, 92

Chopsticks, use of, 67

Cigarettes, 113–14. See also Smoking

Clams, 84–85

Climbing stairs, 22

Clothing, attractiveness and, 166

Coconut oil, 77, 92

Cod (fish), 80

Coffee, 13, 39, 81

Coke (beverage), 20

Cold intolerance, fasting and, 6

Communicating, psychology of weight maintenance and, 168–70

Company gyms, 46–47

Competitive sports, 95, 99, 102–3, 146–48, 172. See also specific kinds

Complex carbohydrates, 39, 73, 81–82, 135; choosing, 81–82; menus, 83–84, 85–87; what they are, 81. See also specific foods

Compulsive eating, 124–28, 133. See also Restrained and unrestrained eating

Constipation, 6, 82; fiber and, 82

Cookbooks, 92

Cookies, 92

Cooking tips, 92–93

Corn, 73, 76

Corn oil, 77, 93

Cottage cheese, 34, 35

Cottonseed oil, 77

Counseling, communication problems and, 169

Crackers, 35, 39, 78, 139

Criticism, 167–68, 169, 170

Cross-country running, 102

Cross-country skiing, 95, 106; machines, 53
Cycling. *See* Bicycling

Daily meal plans, 83–84, 89–90; portion control and, 85–87
Dairy products, 33, 34, 35, 81, 86; fat in, 77, 78, 141. *See also* specific kinds
Dancing, 106; aerobic, 95, 104–5
Dental caries. *See* Cavities
Depression, 125, 126, 127, 135, 159
Desirability attitudes, 167–68
Desserts, 137–38, 158
Diabetes, 5, 30, 45, 136
Dieting, 4–12, 25–71; plateaus, 4, 39, 153–54, 155; psychology of weight maintenance and, 111–30, 156–73; setpoint and, 17–19 (*see also* Setpoint); tapering off from, 25–71. *See also* Fasting; Liquid-protein fast; Obesity; Weight
Diet scale, use of, 31
Dinner, 33, 34–35, 36, 62, 84, 89–90; portion control and, 85–87
Dizziness, 54; fasting and, 6
Doctors: exercise and okay from, 43–45; surgery and, 152–53
Doughnuts, 13, 14, 81, 82, 139
DoveBar, 139
Dry skin, fasting and, 6
Dynamic resistance principle, anaerobic exercise and, 149–52

Eating (food): acceptance of, 10; at home, 38; bites, 138–39, 145; boring, eliminating, 73, 124, 126, 127; calories and (*see* Calories); energy and, 19–24 (*see also* Energy); exercise and, 13–24, 54–55, 94–110; fat content, listed, 78–79 (*see also* Fats, dietary); forbidden, 11, 12, 16 (*see also* Forbidden foods); healthy, 77–94; hunger and satiety and, 56–71 (*see also* Hunger; Satiety); learning how and when to eat, 27–29, 57–71, 72–94; metabolism and, 8–9, 12 (*see also* Metabolism); monitoring weight and, 39–40 (*see also* Weight); new way to think about, 56–71; nighttime, 142–43; out, 38–39 (*see also* Restaurants); pacing (slow), 66–68, 99, 171–72; portion-controlled program and, 72–94; post-fasting program and, 10–12, 13–24, 25–71, 72–94, 110–29 (*see also* Fasting); psychology of weight maintenance and, 111–30, 156–73; replacing liquid-protein diet and, 33–41, 56–71, 72–94, 111–30, 131–45; smell

Eating (*Cont.*): and texture and, 133–44; sweets, desserts, and sugars and, 133–38, 139, 158 (*see also* specific kinds); trigger-food avoidance and, 131–32, 145. *See also* Dieting; Obesity; Weight; specific foods, problems
Egg Beaters, 93
Eggs, 35, 73, 76, 79, 92; substitutes, 93
Embarrassment (self-consciousness), feelings of, 161
Endorphin release, exercise and, 20–21
Energy (energy levels), 6, 8, 16; exercise and, 13–24, 55–56, 89–91, 94–110 (*see also* Exercise); weight and, 18–24, 39, 40–71 *passim*, 88. *See also* Metabolism
Enzymes, setpoint and, 18
Exercise, post-fast program and, 10, 11, 12, 40–71, 94–110, 145–52, 154, 172; additional, rewards and, 146–52, 172; aerobic (*see* Aerobic exercise); anaerobic (*see* Anaerobic exercise); benefits, 13–24, 42–71, 146; body shaping and, 148–52; classes, 51; complementary activities and, 97–99; daily, importance of, 20–24, 45–47; doctor's okay and, 43–45; endorphins and, 20–21; energy expenditure and food intake and, 13–24, 55–56, 89–91, 94–110; evening, 46; exchanges and setpoint, 11, 13–24, 86, 94–110; family contract and, 47–49; frequency and duration of, 99; goals to work for, 11, 145–52, 154, 156, 172; injury prevention and, 106–7, 151; intensity level, 99–100; lowered hunger rating and, 13–24, 42, 46, 55, 68–69; machines (*see* Exercise machines); metabolism and, 14, 17, 19–24, 44; midday, 46–47; mindset and, 42–43; monitoring progress, 107–10; morning, 46; pacing and, 99–100, 111, 129; pain and, 45, 55, 106–7, 146, 147, 151; perceived exertion ratings (PER) and, 97; psychological benefits of (*see under* Psychology); regimens, 100–5; selecting an activity, kinds, 49–52, 95, 111; starting a program and commitment to, 41–71; tapering off the liquid-protein diet and, 41–71; target heart rate and, 97; training level, 96–97, 100; videos (tapes), 50, 52–53; warming up and cooling down and, 54–55, 107. *See also* specific kinds
Exercise bicycle, 46
Exercise machines, 46, 50, 53, 69, 95, 103; anaerobics and, 149–50; cross-country skiing, 53; rowing, 53; stationary, 53, 103; treadmills, 53